Advance Praise for

Purposeful Retirement

"Retirement can easily be an unbelievably bright future for you and your loved ones. You are not a "has been," you are a "will be." Above all, be purposeful. Enjoy all that lies before you!"

– Ken Blanchard, *New York Times* bestselling author of *The One Minute Manager* and *Refire, Don't Retire*

"I agree wholeheartedly with Hyrum Smith: you may be retired, but you can still live with meaning, purpose and energy."

- Marshall Goldsmith, executive coach, business educator and *New York Times* bestselling author of *Mojo*

PURPOSEFUL RETIREMENT

How to Bring Happiness and Meaning to Your Retirement

HYRUM W. SMITH

Bestselling Author of
*The 10 Natural Laws of Successful Time
and Life Management*

For permission requests, please contact the publisher at:

Mango Publishing Group
2850 Douglas Road, 3rd Floor
Coral Gables, FL 33134 USA
info@mango.bz

For special orders, quantity sales, course adoptions and corporate sales, please email the publisher at sales@mango.bz. For trade and wholesale sales, please contact Ingram Publisher Services at customer.service@ingramcontent.com or +1.800.509.4887.

PURPOSEFUL RETIREMENT:
How to Bring Happiness and Meaning to Your Retirement.

Library of Congress Cataloging-in-Publication has been applied for.

ISBN: (hardcover) 978-1-63353-503-9, (ebook) 978-1-63353-502-2

Printed in the United States of America

"Age is an issue of mind over matter.
If you don't mind, it doesn't matter."

-Mark Twain

Table of Contents

PURPOSEFUL
RETIREMENT

Foreword

What's next?

That's a profound question we will all need to answer as we move into the last third of our lives. This timely and insightful book by Hyrum Smith will help us develop our response to this important, unavoidable, and potentially inspiring question.

As Hyrum mentions in his author's preface, he's not retired—at least not in the traditional definition of retiring from a life of work and contribution to a stage of leisure and idle accumulation. My father, Stephen R. Covey, strongly believed the same. His advice to his family, and to the world, was to live life in crescendo! In other words, believe that your greatest contribution is always ahead of you. You might retire from a job—but never retire from making contributions. Indeed, life is about contribution, not accumulation. Hyrum admirably exemplifies this wisdom in his life and in this book.

I came to know Hyrum very well when we merged Covey Leadership Center, the company founded by my father, with Franklin Quest, the company Hyrum established. I was serving as the President and CEO of Covey Leadership Center at the time and continued on with the newly merged company, FranklinCovey Co. I found in Hyrum an absolutely fascinating person who embodies purpose and passion. And what

I learned quickly was that one of Hyrum's greatest qualities is his extremely generous nature.

Soon after the merger was completed, Hyrum and his kind wife, Gail, invited my wife, Jeri, and me to their spacious ranch in southern Utah. They were such hospitable hosts and they made us feel so special throughout our stay. I thought this was something unique to us because of our significant business relationship only to discover later that this was the way Hyrum and Gail treated everyone. Indeed they have hosted hundreds, if not thousands, of people at their ranch (it was rumored that some people actually lived on the ranch for years!). Hyrum genuinely seeks to make a difference in the world through his amazing gifts and talents.

As you read this book, you will likely find your existing ideas about retirement challenged. Hyrum will stretch your comfort zone in his incomparable way. Know that this book is not for everyone. If retirement for you is whiling away your hours in leisure, you probably won't enjoy this read. You will find that Hyrum will cajole—and inspire—you to make more of your years ahead.

There are three things I think you'll really value about this book.

First, what you'll find in here is a lifetime's worth of wisdom and experience from a straight-shooting storyteller who practices what he preaches. With Hyrum, what you see is what you get. Take the time to savor his insights in each chapter. Then respond to each of the "Purposeful Planning Questions" that spur reflection—and action. This is not just a light scattering of ideas—it's very hands-on and deserves not only reading, but implementation.

Second, this wisdom is supported by examples from interesting people Hyrum has met and interviewed, and some he has known for decades. Their experiences inform and support the ideas and suggestions presented and give a real hope and possibility that you can do this too, as well as the cautionary tales of those who've not retired purposefully.

Third, and the most fun, is Hyrum's sense of humor. It shines through on almost every page, whether it's in stories from his remarkable life or amusing sidebars he's collected through the years. I won't be surprised if you laugh out loud at some of them—I certainly did! And if you ever have an opportunity to hear him speak in a live setting, take it. Hyrum is absolutely one of the most engaging and powerful storytellers I've ever heard.

I predict Hyrum's purpose and passion for life will inspire you. From my years of working with leaders and organizations to increase trust, there is a great need for each of us to make a unique contribution to improve the world.

Hyrum's fundamental challenge is to encourage you to develop confidence in your new identity in this new stage of life. In other words, it's an inspired invitation to trust yourself for the purpose of making new contributions and creating a better world where people trust wisely.

I hope you enjoy your journey of exploring "what's next". Indeed, the rest of your life can be the best of your life!

Stephen M. R. Covey
Co-founder & Global Practice Leader of FranklinCovey's Speed of Trust Practice, Author of *The Speed of Trust* and *Smart Trust*

Preface

When it comes to writing, there is one cardinal rule: you write what you know. Understanding this rule, I am going to confess here in this Author's Preface just one thing. I wrote this book on creating a Purposeful Retirement, but I am not retired. At least not in the way it is traditionally defined and has been traditionally lived. I'm way too busy for that.

I'm still writing, I'm still teaching seminars all over the country, I'm still volunteering my time to wonderful programs and projects. I'm still trying to make a difference in this world.

I am not retired. I'm not done yet. And I'm certainly not dead yet. I'm just doing something else. And it's great!

Within these pages, you will not find hints on how to improve your shuffleboard game. I am not going to list restaurants for you that offer 'Early Dining' specials. And I'm definitely not going to tell you how to make the most of your Netflix subscription.

But I am going to provide some suggestions on how to create and live a purposeful retirement that brings you joy.

Retirees all around you are living longer. And we're living better! Retirement is no longer an end. It's a new season to live purposefully.

Don't retire! Join me in just doing something else. If you're ready to create a purposeful retirement, read this book. Take note of the stories and suggestions that ring true to you. Take away some ideas. Make plans today. Because we're not done and we're definitely not dead yet!

Introduction:
A State of Being
"von Bismarcked"

"Retirement at sixty-five is ridiculous. When I was sixty-five I still had pimples."
- George Burns

In 1881, Otto von Bismarck, Chancellor over Prussia and later a modern, unified Germany, announced a shocking initiative. He proposed that everyone over the age of 70 should receive government assistance.

His announcement was both perfectly radical and perfectly conservative, probably satisfying no one in 1881. The initiative was radical in that nothing so sweeping had been done before. Yes, military pensions were in place, and in the United States the government paid some municipal employees, such as firefighters, police officers, and teachers public pensions.

But von Bismarck's proposal, which took eight years to be passed into law, was sweeping in its enormity. No one had ever considered giving people money to not work. For thousands of years, you worked until you died. If you were wealthy, you were lucky.

The proposal was actually conservative as well. It was 1881, after all. If you were born at that time, you could expect to live to the ripe old age of 40 if you were male and 56 if you were female.

So the proposal had the ability to affect tens upon tens of people. It was a promise people missed by at least a few decades, though von Bismarck himself was 66 when he first introduced the idea.

The only thing von Bismarck did not do in 1881 was name it after himself or we might all be living in a state of being "von Bismarcked." But that would lead to a problem Shakespeare himself warned us about. Would retirement by any other name depress as many people?

The word retirement has a somewhat negative connotation because it is associated with being an end of something, in this case a significant and lifelong journey.

Don't end. Don't be von Bismarck-ed.

I'm in my 70s, and I will be the first to tell you I am not traditionally "retired." I am just doing something else. I've just changed my daily scenery. Retirement is final. Retirement is the end. I'm nowhere near my end. How about you?

I was recently buying corn at a farmer's market, picking out prize cobs, when I struck up a conversation with a gentleman next to me who was probably my age but looked much older, of course. He was bemoaning the ridiculousness of retirement. He did not do what was expected and retire promptly at

65. He held on a few more years, which made sense to him.

"I not only knew how to do everything," he said, "But I knew why. I was the institutional memory, and you can't just replace that. Why should you think of replacing that just because someone reaches the number 65? That's stupid. That's shooting your business in the foot."

My farmer's market acquaintance is not the only person who considers retirement to be an almost unnatural state. Author Mary-Lou Weisman wrote a satirical article for the *New York Times* outlining "The History of Retirement."

In the beginning, there was no retirement. There were no old people. In the Stone Age, everyone was fully employed until age 20, by which time nearly everyone was dead, usually of unnatural causes. Any early man who lived long enough to develop crow's-feet was either worshiped or eaten as a sign of respect. Even in Biblical times, when a fair number of people made it into old age, retirement still had not been invented and respect for old people remained high. In those days, it was customary to carry on until you dropped, regardless of your age group -- no shuffleboard, no Airstream trailer. When a patriarch could no longer farm, herd cattle, or pitch a tent, he opted for more specialized, less labor-intensive work, like prophesying and handing down commandments. Or he moved in with his kids.

As the centuries passed, the elderly population increased. By early medieval times, their numbers had reached critical mass. It was no longer just a matter of respecting the occasional white-bearded patriarch. Old people were everywhere, giving advice, repeating themselves, complaining about rheumatism, trying to help, getting in the way, and making younger people feel guilty. Plus they tended to hang on to their wealth and property.

> By 1935, it became evident that the only way to get old people to stop working for pay was to pay them enough to stop working. . . . The opposite of work turned out to be play. The rich discovered leisure first, but by 1910, Florida became accessible to the middle class. Retirement communities, where older people did not have to see younger people working, began to appear in the 1920's and 30's. The number of golf courses in the United States tripled between 1921 and 1930. Subsequent technological developments like movies and television helped turn having nothing to do into a leisure time activity. From now on, the elderly would work at play.

Clearly, Weisman's words are satire, but she strikes on an idea that rings true to some people: retirement is an unnatural, modern invention. It's a weird little creation von Bismarck came up with. And now tradition dictates that someone gets to tell us to stop working simply because we arrive at a certain age.

"It's ridiculous!" you might say. Then don't stop. I'm not going to let someone hand me a Social Security check and shoo me away. I am going to treat retirement as **my time**. I am going to ensure I make a difference with the time I am given.

What about you?

- Maybe you want to start a new business.

- Maybe you want to fulfill your dream of being a DJ.

- Maybe you want to be a greeter at Wal-Mart and have an excuse to talk to people all day long and even get paid for it!

- Maybe you want to take tickets at a movie theater or help people find their seats as an usher at a play.

- Maybe you want to go on multiple adventures with your spouse.

- Maybe you want to ride bicycles with your grandkids.

- Maybe you want to try something you have never done before.

Pick a maybe!

Now is the time to consider all options, because now you finally have time to consider all options. If you're ready to plan a purposeful retirement, I have some suggestions. Let's talk about it.

Chapter 1

Two Camps

C onor O'Reilly was a good Irishman. And because
he was a good Irishman, with the sun setting on
a Friday evening, he found himself in his car, driving
down the barely paved road that led to his favorite
local pub.

It had been a long week. Just the thought of sitting
with his favorite drink around a crowded table with
some of his favorite blokes, and suddenly the world
looked as though it might right itself just fine before
another week began.

At the end of his path, Conor began the search for a
parking spot. Parking outside of this particular pub
was always difficult. The fact that it was Friday night
made it more so. Conor circled around once. Twice. A
parking spot was nowhere to be found.

> "Men do not quit playing because they grow
> old; they grow old because they quit playing."
> **- Oliver Wendell Holmes**

Unwilling to give up and drive home, Conor looked up
toward heaven and offered a most fervent prayer.

"Lord, if you grant me a parking space, I'll go to
Church every Sunday like a good Irish Catholic
should."

Low and behold, a space miraculously opened up
right in front of him! Greatly relieved, Conor looked

back up toward heaven and said, "Never mind, Lord, I found one!"

We may all conclude that Conor was granted a heavenly gift. But he did not see it that way. We can, and should, laugh at Conor's story. But then we should realize that sometimes in our lives, we are all Conor. Sometimes in our lives, we are all given gifts. Some we ignore. Some we've asked for and happily receive. Others stun and confuse us.

"What am I supposed to do with this?"

How many times have we thought this as we opened a gift we did not ask for and did not really want? I'm talking about more than cat sweaters and lime green knitted pot holders. I'm also talking about retirement.

The Gift Of Retirement

Retirement can be a gift — a gift that opens up right in front of us like a perfect parking spot. It's a gift of time and a gift of opportunities. But, unlike Conor, we must first recognize it.

If we were sitting together, perhaps at Conor's pub, I would ask you about the very beginning of your own retirement. If I had to guess, I would assume you ate a cake with too much frosting in the conference room. You probably offered up several hugs, some genuine, some a little awkward. At the end of the day, you shut down your computer and packed up your bag one last time.

On the way out, did you turn out the light? And, because you could not help yourself, did you look back over your shoulder? Just one last time?

As you walked out that door, you realized you were done. You've officially joined the retired ranks!

So tell me. Out of the two retirement camps, which one do you fall in? It has been my experience that in Camp One you'll find people who have been planning and looking forward to retirement since the day they started their first real job. As they have gotten closer to THE DAY, they've inserted a countdown as a screensaver on their work computer. And on the day they retire, they nearly dance out the door.

And in Camp Two there are people who "do not go gentle into that good night." They go out the door kicking and screaming, their fingers tightly gripping the door jamb of their office because retirement looms before them like an empty abyss.

"Age is an issue of mind over matter. If you don't mind, it doesn't matter."
– Mark Twain

Picking Your Camp

So, back to my question. What camp are you? Where are you pitching your tent? Are you dancing the retirement jig? Did you run toward that exit door? Or are you in the other camp? Did you fight it tooth and nail?

And how does that affect the rest of your retirement? Are you happy? Or are you looking around and wondering, "How did I get here?" In other words, did you open that gift of retirement and think: "What am I supposed to do with this?"

No matter the camp, no matter how you got here, now that you are here, I have just one thing to say:

Don't just retire. Don't you dare check out and just retire.

Why? Because people who retire die. It's an absolute fact. Researchers took a look at employees of a global oil company who chose to retire early at 55 and compared them to employees who retired at the traditional age of 65. The study found those who retired early died sooner. The early retirees had a 37 percent higher risk of death and those that died at 55 were 89 percent more likely to die in the 10 years after retirement than those who retired at 65.

So don't just retire.

 "Wait!" I can hear you scream. "I've already retired!"

Technically, that's true. And that's fine. In fact, it just might be great.

Just don't retire from living.

Just don't end.

Take this gift of time. Take this gift of opportunity. Take this gift and redirect your life. Take this gift and purposefully redirect your retirement.

You've left your day job and perhaps even turned off your alarm clock. But that doesn't mean it's time to grab a crocheted blanket, wear down your favorite recliner and start shouting out "What is" answers to Alex Trebek. In fact, I think all new retirees need to spend the first four days of their retirement in front of the television for 18 hours straight. They'll never make that mistake again. It'll be so miserable they'll get up and get moving.

Take this gift of time and choose to do so much more.

Perhaps:

- Now is the time to launch a new career — the one you always wanted to do but couldn't because you needed a predictable paycheck.

- Now is the time to focus on your family.

- Now is the time to make a difference in your community.

As I mentioned earlier, now is the time because now you have time.

The Stress of Doing Nothing

I once met a heart surgeon who had had a heart attack. Professionally, that can really ruin your reputation. Instead of ignoring what he had gone through, he began studying the physical effects of stress.

> *"A lot of our friends complain about their retirement. We tell 'em to get a life."*
> **– Larry Laser**

Around the same time, 1987 to be exact, the stock market crashed. Many of us remember the shock of Black Monday more vividly than we remember what we ate yesterday. It was a dark and frightening time.

One company in particular experienced both financial and personal losses attributed to Black Monday. The company hired this surgeon to come in as a coach and teach their employees how to reduce stress and hopefully save their lives.

This surgeon told those employees that there are essentially two types of reactions to stress. One kind of reaction is actually healthy. He called it cool stress. Cool stress can help us function better and will help us respond in a positive manner.

Psychologists refer to cool stress as "eustress." It's the type of stress we feel when we are excited and happy. Remember riding a favorite roller coaster ride and going over that first big hill? As you climbed into the sky, your pulse quickened. This is eustress. You feel alive and excited.

And then there's hot stress, referred to as "distress." Hot stress is damaging. Your heart beats faster, which sends more blood into your arteries. You have more blood being pushed through the body at a faster rate. But unfortunately, your body also reacts to hot stress by contracting your blood vessels. More and more blood is trying to course through a smaller and smaller hole. Your heart works overtime. Your entire cardiovascular system becomes worn down. Your blood pressure goes up, and you could experience a stroke or heart attack. In the short term, you are cranky, experience a lack of energy, and may suffer from headaches or stomach ulcers, bouts of insomnia, and weight gain.

Are there tricks to reducing hot stress? Sure. In fact, entire books have been written about how to do just that. This book is not one of those. But decades ago I wanted to know more, too. I discovered that this surgeon put people through tests to see what type of stress their bodies produced. He invited me to participate, and I spent a day and a half going through these tests.

I played Pong Games. I got on a treadmill. I had to stick my hand in ice until I could not take it any longer. By the way, that hurt like hell. Toward the end of the day, I was sitting alone in a room, hooked up to machines, waiting for more torture to come my way.

"We're going to leave you hooked up for a minute," I was told. "Just relax. We'll come back in and unhook you in about ten minutes."

I sat there for a few minutes, and sure enough, they came along and unhooked me from the machines which had been monitoring my stress levels throughout the whole experience.

The next day I was invited to come in and review my stress findings with several doctors. As I walked into the office, I saw my stress readings were recorded on several pages, all folded up.

"Hyrum, you have the coolest reactions to stress I have ever tested," said one of the doctors. He turned page after page and I saw little movement in the recording – until the end, where the needle recording went off the charts. Was that when I was playing video games? On the treadmill? Sticking my hand in ice until the pain nearly put me in the fetal position?

No.

"This line here," the doctor said, "This is where we suggested that you relax. You rejected the suggestion. Your body totally rejected the idea of sitting there and doing nothing."

Once home, I reported the findings to my wife, and she laughed.

"Oh, that's so true!" she said. "You're awful! We go on vacation, and you clean! You always have to do something. You do not know how to relax. You do not know how to sit still!"

For some, that's the problem with retirement. There's nothing to do. And we are used to being busy to the point of addiction, a gnawing need. So we garden. We paint. We even clean the garage. But what do we do when we look around and it's all done? We have all this time and are not sure what to do with it. It feels almost unnatural.

The purpose of this book is not to help you write a 30 page plan for your retirement or even give you some financial advice on how to make the most of your retirement dollars. The purpose of this book is to get you to start thinking about options for your retirement and hopefully put together a plan – be it formal or informal – for retirement, and have that plan make a purposeful difference in your life and in the lives of those around you.

Purposeful Planning Questions:

1. What camp are you in?

2. How does your camp continue to shape your views on retirement?

3. Since retirement is a gift, who can you share that gift with today?

4. Is there a friend, grandchild, younger person who needs your time?

Chapter 2

Turning In the Title

Stripped of your job title, who are you?

When George Bush lost to Bill Clinton in the election of 1992, George and Barbara Bush left the White House in Washington, D.C. and moved to Texas. Barbara Bush shared that tough adjustment in her book, *Reflections: Life After The White House.*

> Our days were spent getting used to being back on our own, living in a rented house with two dogs after four years in that glorious house with ninety-three staff. We realized fairly quickly how much life had changed. George W. came for dinner a few days after our return home. He wanted pasta, as he was running the Houston Marathon the next morning. I had not cooked in twelve years, so it was not surprising that my pasta was NOT too good. In fact, it was dreadful. George W. was polite, but his dad said, "I like my pasta rare." By that time, I had cooked about five meals, and I figured I was two for five. George told me the good news was that he had lost two pounds without even trying.

> One weekend we went to Galveston – just a short hour's drive from Houston on the Gulf of Mexico – and stayed in our friend Hugh Liedtke's house on the water. When George went in to get a fishing license, the woman said to him, "You look familiar. Have we met before?"

Something very similar happened to me, although a little while later. My good friend and neighbor, Mildred Kerr, and I went to Luby's Cafeteria for lunch. A perfectly strange, attractive woman came over, put her face in mine, and said, "Aren't you somebody? I know I know you." She never took a breath and continued, "Are you a teacher? Have you waited on me in a store? Did you help me at Sears?" I never had a chance to say a word, but just kept nodding. She left as quickly as she arrived, muttering as she went: "I thought she was somebody."

Aren't You Somebody?

Aren't you somebody? Don't we all fear that question?

We do an odd thing as a society when we meet someone new. We stretch out our hand. We offer up a name, perhaps the approximate location of where we live, and promptly attach to that a job title.

"Hello. My name is Kaden Buchler. I live around the corner in Springdale, where I work as an attorney."

"Hi! My name is Bailey Michelsen. I live down south from here in Pineview. I'm a professor at the university."

And on we go. I believe that's what makes people nervous about retirement. It's a fear of losing a part of ourselves, a part of our identity.

Ridiculous. You are more than a fancy job title. You have value simply by being a human being. You've always had this value and you always will.

A friend of mine, Steven Baugh, worked in a prominent position in his county government and then went on to teach at a large university. He told me, "I know people who fear being forgotten after they retire. I always say you go from a 'who's who' to a 'who's he?' And it's frightening."

This fear is a natural one. We all have egos. Just when I am excessively proud of my level of humility, I realize I need to go back and perhaps check my ego again. The danger comes when we allow ourselves to be defined by our job, our title, and the size of our paycheck. The danger comes when we ask, 'When it is gone, what is left?'

You are. You are left. You, with your skill, talent, and ability to make a difference. You.

From Professor To Mrs.

When she left her position as a professor in order to battle cancer, Ann Barnes went from being 'Professor Barnes' to 'Mrs. Barnes.' It was a hard adjustment.

"I love being married, but Mrs. Barnes is not how I refer to myself. It was an adjustment for me, especially as a woman, because it was an accomplishment to reach and become established at that level. It was a distinguishing characteristic because it was unusual for my generation. Today, we expect our daughters and granddaughters to establish themselves and take advantage of opportunities in education, but for my generation, it was not the norm. I think it makes it harder to let go of it," she said.

Leaving that identity behind caused a physical ache, she admitted. "It's a part of you, a prominent side of you. Walking away from that is tough. But it is not the end. Retirement gives you an opportunity to focus on things that are really important."

When she felt well enough to travel, Ann and her husband took a cruise around the world. A year later, they toured Cuba. Just a few weeks ago, they headed off to Mexico.

> "Today we are doing all the things we always
> wanted to do. Change can be a good thing, and
> that is what retirement is – a really big change."

Ann is right. This season called retirement is a big change. Life is full of changes. When we are no longer students, we adjust and change. When we choose to leave a career to raise a family, we adjust and change. When our last child leaves for college and we are left with an empty nest, we adjust and change. When we retire, it's one more change. Shouldn't we be used to them by now? Shouldn't we be experts at them by now?

I briefly introduced my friend Steven Baugh a few paragraphs ago. When we were talking about retirement, Steven explained that retirement "is just one more level of adjustment. I compare it to when my wife was raising our kids. She told me that she still had a brain. She still had skills. She still had abilities. She wanted the validation for all of those things. I think the same is true of people who are retired. We still have a brain. We still have skills. We still have abilities. We still want the validation."

We still want people to know we are somebody.

I built up a company. It now employs thousands of people. But I know if I walked in the door, chances are the person sitting at the front desk would not recognize me. If I walked down the hall, there would be a lot of faces I would not recognize. Even under the roof of my own company, I could argue that I have gone from a who's who to who's he.

I don't worry about it. I choose to not let it bother me. The older some people get, the more obsessed they become with the idea of being remembered. So let me take some of the stress off of you and share this simple truth with you: the people who really matter to you will never forget you. Period.

Your close friends, your family, the people you love – all of these people will never forget you. And the people at work? Yes, maybe they'll forget you because you never mattered to them in the first place. So why spend one iota of time worrying about them? The fact is that the people who forget you are not the people that matter to you. Your focus, your purpose, must be on the people that do.

Your Belief Window

As you're thinking about the titleless you, let's talk about your Belief Window. You have one. Everyone has one. It's right in front of you. You move, it moves. It's always with you. It hangs in front of your face. It's a storage place for all of the principles you believe to be true.

Now, whether they are true or not is another issue. You think they are correct. That's why they are there – because we believe they are true. If my Belief Window is full of correct principles, I will have a good life. If not, if I have incorrect principles on my Belief Window, then my behavior will be based on beliefs that will not work for me over time. In fact, they will make my life very uncomfortable.

For example, if I believe gravity only works part of the time, that's a problem. I really need to correct that.

Some of the beliefs on your window are true and some are false. Some are good, some are not. Some are rational, others are irrational.

I am not referring to spiritual beliefs. I am referring to deductions you may have made in your life and smacked onto your belief window, such as:

- Roller skating always leads to broken arms;

- Ford is a reliable brand;

- Green food is bad.

As you see your world through your Belief Window, it affects every thought of every day. And if you change your principles on your Belief Window, you can change your life.

The number of principles on your Belief Window is a function of your age and experience. Your own Belief Window by now is probably excessively crowded. It's a wonder you can still see through it. All these beliefs influence your behavior.

- You may shy away from roller skating and not teach or encourage your children or grandchildren how to skate.

- You may only go to a Ford dealership when shopping for a new vehicle.

- You may choose to skip the salad bar at a restaurant.

You place beliefs on your Belief Window because they fill a need for you as you figure out the world around you. If you want to change your life, you need to start by changing your Belief Window because your actions – your life being the sum of them – are all based on your Belief Window.

You can choose to recognize a certain result in your life, trace it back to a belief on your Belief Window and ask, "Do the results of a particular principle or belief on my Belief Window meet my needs over time?" If not, you have an incorrect or inadequate belief on your Belief Window. You need to replace it.

Let's consider a set of applicable beliefs which may be on your Belief Window:

1. Unemployed people are lazy.

2. Personal value only comes through hard work.

3. Important people have important titles.

4. If I am busy, I am important.

These statements may be on your Belief Window. They control the way you see your world and, more importantly, how you see your retirement. What happens to you if this is how you see your world when you retire? What happens to you if these principles are on your Belief Window?

Let's consider the first one: **unemployed people are lazy**. Guess what! You're essentially unemployed. Does that mean you are lazy? How does that translate in the way you act? In the way you treat yourself and speak to yourself? Have you allowed yourself to become lazy because it matches a Belief on your Belief Window? Well, stop it!

> *"Rest is not idleness, and to lie sometimes on the grass under trees on a summer's day, listening to the murmur of the water, or watching the clouds float across the sky, is by no means a waste of time."*
> **– J. Lubbock**

Or the second one, **personal value only comes through hard work**. I have a friend who retired after a stressful and highly productive career. When he worked, he missed many family activities. "But it was understood I was needed at work, so there was little guilt associated with missing family events," he said. But when he retired, family members expected him at all family events because, well, 'what else did he have to do?' they wondered.

"When I retired, I really struggled with the demands of my family on my time. Events and social gatherings seemed to grow exponentially, and I got frustrated. I was a checklist guy. I wanted to check things off, and when my time was being scheduled by other people -- also known as my kids -- I was frustrated by the expectation that I would always be there. These events were stopping me from getting anything done!"

Personal value only comes from hard work was on his Belief Window, and spending time with family was not a valuable substitute. My friend needed to go back and consciously remove that principle of thought from his Belief Window.

How about the third one? **Important people have important titles**. If that's on my Belief Window, if my value is linked to my job, then when I leave my job, I am done. I am just done. The emotional response can be powerful. Can you feel it? Can you relate to it? If you believe your job is the only thing which gives you value, you are done the minute you walk out of that office door.

I once gave a presentation on the Belief Window concept and on how to change your life by changing the beliefs on your Belief Window. A gentleman came up to me when it was all over. He introduced himself, and he emotionally told me he was a retired American Airlines pilot.

"When they took those wings off my chest, something collapsed inside of me," he shared. "I don't know who I am. I cannot tell people that I am a pilot anymore, and that is what I have felt, for decades, gave me value. I have to change my Belief Window. I have to change what gives me value."

My value as a human being is independent of my job. If I based my value on my job and my job goes away, my value as a human goes away with it. This leads to big trouble. This leads to unhappiness, isolation, depression, and eventually death.

The minute you find value from just being you, you will find inner peace. But first you must not only understand but you must know your value has nothing to do with your job title.

We all must decide, "Wherein do I have value?"

Your answer should be: just you. What gives you value is just who you are. If your Belief Window acknowledges value simply because you are human, then when you retire, you can go on to the next season in life and be very satisfied and happy.

The need to feel important makes us do a lot of dumb things. If I believe that doing 'stuff' gives me value because I feel validated by all these people watching me do this 'stuff', I will overwhelm myself. It will not work for me over time. Whenever my self-worth is dependent on anything or anyone external from me, I am in trouble.

Finally, let's take a look at the last belief on the Belief Window: **if I am busy, I am important.**

"There can be a bereft feeling when you retire," my friend Lynn Snow shared with me. He worked for decades as a CPA and then as a real estate broker and developer, in addition to serving on the city planning and zoning board in his community. "I miss the engagement and the challenges." Though retired, he still stays on top of the latest technology in his field. A few months ago he heard about an update to a bookkeeping software tool, and so he purchased the program and started taking online courses to learn about the new program.

"Why do you have to do that?" a neighbor asked him. "You're retired!"

"I don't have to," Lynn explained. "I just want to."

"I do not want to go back to it," he clarified. "But sometimes I miss it. When I retired, I found myself asking, 'What am I going to do now?'"

So Lynn found an answer to that question: What am I going to do now? He started to volunteer at his church. He likes helping people with genealogy, and so he began to work in a genealogy center as a volunteer. He works with the Boy Scouts of America. "I am retired," Lynn said, "But I still believe that I should contribute. And I try to."

Lynn has friends who have dreaded retirement. "They do not know what they want to do," he shared. They may have two of the beliefs we just discussed on their own Belief Window:

1. Unemployed people are lazy.

2. Personal value only comes through hard work.

The very act of being retired is upsetting to them. I understand this feeling of anxiety. When I was young, I thought that I needed to be active, I thought I needed to be busy to be important. If I was ever sitting down in my house, my father would enter the room and ask, "What are you doing to justify your existence?"

I discovered that as long as I was moving, as long as I was perpetually in motion, I was validated. For me, busyness was validating.

It was a curse, but I found how to counteract it.

Stop being busy. Start being productive.

When you feel productive, you feel great at the end of the day. If you spent your entire day centered around busy work, you were not productive, and you will feel it. You spent the day without direction and without any clear goals. You don't feel good about what you did that day. The best litmus test for productivity is to ask yourself, "What did I do today? How did I acomplish today?"

Daily planning gives you a shield against being lost in busyness. It takes you out of the busy world and into the productive world.

Let's say it's a quiet Monday morning. In planning my day, I have decided to prune a particularly aggressive apple tree that's growing on my ranch. As I'm setting out, I hear the slight "bing!" of my phone announcing a new email. If I didn't have a plan, I'd stop. I'd check the email and realize it was from Zalmonzo Furniture Store offering me a 20 percent-off coupon. Intrigued, I would scroll down the email, looking at all of the options and the new sale prices. And twenty minutes later, well, twenty minutes later I'd realize I'd wasted twenty minutes. And then I'd hear another "bing!" And it would start all over again. I could easily spend an entire morning lost in Zalmonzo emails.

But I do have a daily plan; and it keeps me productive. Not busy. Productive. In my daily plan, I set aside one hour every day to check my email and read articles which may come into my inbox. It helps me not get lost in a false reality, in a sea of Zalmonzo coupons. It helps me stay proactive and not reactive, something I've written about extensively in other books.

If I have a daily plan, I am proactive. If I do not have a plan, I will be reactive to whatever comes my way throughout the day. I'll be busy, but at the end of the day, I'll recognize that today was not a day that mattered, and I will be unsatisfied.

If I am proactive, I will feel that I made a difference. Getting from reactive to proactive is a journey. This journey will help you manage your time and help you make good choices as you script your day. And then you're going to experience an "Aha!" moment. In fact, you're going to experience what I call a BFO, a "Blinding Flash of the Obvious" moment when you realize that time management is truly management.

It is putting what matters most to you in line and as the focus of your day. And then you'll experience inner peace. That's the quest of time management. That's where we start really managing our lives and getting our lives back, because we are deciding what events matter and putting those events in sequence in a manner which makes sense to us and not letting other things get in the way.

I met a man, retired Air Force Colonel Kenneth Page, who was a little lost when he retired. "I found that if

I did not have a specific plan for what I wanted to do on a day-to-day basis, I would not get much done. I no longer had deadlines. I no longer had meetings. What was I going to do? What was my plan? I still wanted a plan for each and every day," he said.

Colonel Page also had to redefine what it meant to be productive. "At work, that is easy to define, but in retirement, it is totally different. Yes, you can complete a 'honey-do' list. Or you can work on projects which you create. But is that productive? Maybe, but often not. Almost every day I found myself hoping and planning and praying for a productive day. I did not want to waste my time. And I also realized that without a plan in mind, things came up. These 'things' grew in number and demanded my attention. My time was filled with these things."

The option is clear: either you consciously plan and decide how you want to fill your time and act purposefully or you allow outside forces to fill your time for you.

Starting tomorrow, how do you plan your time to ensure you're productive and not just busy?

Go beyond asking yourself:

- What am I going to do today?

- What am I going to do this week?

Go deeper and ask:

- How am I going to make a difference?

But before you answer those questions, you must first understand who you are and what matters to you.

Purposeful Planning Questions:

1. What principles regarding retirement are on your Belief Window?

2. How do these principles control the way you perceive retirement?

3. Consider your life the last seven days. Were you proactive or reactive?

4. How can daily planning help you be more proactive in your retirement?

5. Write out a daily plan for tomorrow.

Chapter 3

Discovered Values,
Directed Time

BJ Gallagher, a popular keynote speaker and author of more than 30 books, recently said to me, "Retirement isn't for me." She's the right age. Her hair is the right color. Her ability to participate in early bird dining is unfettered. But she's decided a traditional retirement is not how she wants to spend this season of her life.

"I peer ahead into the final third of my life and wonder, 'What's next? How do I want to spend my final two or three decades?' The one thing I know for sure is that retirement isn't **for me**. Old age isn't **for me**. Being an old lady isn't **for me**. Because unless my life is lived for others, it doesn't seem worthwhile. I want my old age to be about giving, not getting."

BJ has decided that her retirement is not going to be all about her. It's going to be about others. Because that is her focus, she has decided that her time and her retirement are going to be directed toward others.

"Retirement is not for **me**. It's for the people I can serve," she said. "It's for the friends and family I can help and the younger generations I can teach. Now is the time for me to pass along what has so generously been given to me."

I firmly believe that the assumption that everyone wants to make a difference — like BJ — is a valid assumption. And this focus can change your entire retirement.

"If you want happiness for an hour, take a nap.
If you want happiness for a day, go fishing.
If you want happiness for a year, inherit a fortune.
If you want happiness for a lifetime, help somebody."
– Chinese Proverb

If people feel they are making a difference, they are happier. Chances are, you've felt this in your own life. In an article by Jenny Santi for Time Magazine, I read that science is starting to prove this as well. Santi wrote:

> Through MRI technology, we now know that giving activates the same parts of the brain that are stimulated by food and sex. Experiments show evidence that altruism is hardwired in the brain— and it's pleasurable. Helping others may just be the secret to living a life that is not only happier but also healthier, wealthier, more productive, and meaningful.

If people feel they are making a difference, they want to get out of bed in the morning. People who volunteer have a higher level of self-esteem and overall well-being. They feel connected to the world around them. They benefit from a feeling of community and feel less lonely and isolated.

And yes, I believe that if people feel they are making a difference, they live longer, for no bigger reason than the fact that they have something to live for.

A study published in BMC Public Health concluded that taking time to volunteer — by serving in a soup kitchen or reading to others — could reduce early mortality rates by 22 percent, compared to those who do not volunteer.

"Our systematic review shows that volunteering is associated with improvements in health," lead author Dr. Suzanne Richards of the University of Exeter Medical School in England wrote.

How do you start? How do you create a purposeful retirement? How do you begin to make a difference? You begin by taking the time to figure out what matters the most to you. You do that by defining your own personal constitution.

"Unless life is lived for others, it is not worthwhile."
– Mother Teresa

A Personal Constitution

The U.S. federal constitution is a guideline for the governance of the country. It sets the parameters for action for our judicial, legislative and executive branches.

What controls the parameters of the actions you take? Hopefully it's your values.

Everyone has a set of governing values. These values identify the highest priorities in our lives, and they govern how we choose to live our lives. When presented with competing and conflicting options, our governing values help us live the life we want to live.

How do you identify these governing values? You start by identifying what matters most to you. You start by putting yourself on an I-beam.

The I-Beam Question

An I-beam is vital in construction, especially in large buildings like skyscrapers. I-beams are normally made out of structural steel. Though only six inches wide, they are strong, long beams that can carry and support tremendous weight and are utilized to frame out buildings.

Do you have a picture of an I-beam in mind? I want you to imagine a particularly long I-beam, about 300 feet long or essentially the length of a football field. If an I-beam was stretched out on the ground and I asked you to walk the length of it for $100, I think you would make the walk. If you fell, well, your feet would immediately touch the ground and no harm would be done. And if you made it across, you just earned $100, which is not a bad reward for a 300 foot walk.

But what if it was placed over the north rim of the Grand Canyon? Now, a single misstep would mean falling 1,160 feet straight down. If I offered you $100, would you make the walk across the I-beam?

I am guessing that 99.99 percent of all people would respond, "No, thank you." They would think I was insane for even making the offer.

But now put yourself back at the Grand Canyon. It's hot and windy. You are on one side of the canyon, and I'm on the other. But I'm not alone. Looking across the deep divide, you see a beloved grandchild on the opposite side with me. I'm no longer a nice guy handing out $100 bills. I'm a monster, and I'm holding your grandchild over the abyss. The only way to reach me, to stop me, is to cross that I-beam, six inches wide, 300 feet across. Would you step onto the I-beam? Would you do everything you could to make it to the other side?

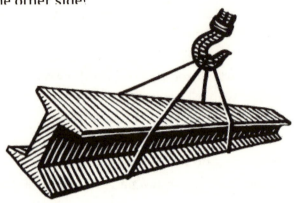

I've literally asked this question all over the world. And the answer always comes swiftly back, "Yes, of course I would." Because you value family, because you value that grandchild, you'll take that step.

By changing the reward, we have found a governing value. Your governing values are your highest, deepest, most valued priorities in your life. These values are who you are, and they identify what makes you – you.

Your governing values are your answers to the question: **what would I cross the I-beam for?**

I would assume you would cross the I-beam for your family. You would cross the I-beam for good health. You might even cross the I-beam for future educational pursuits. **You** decide what you would cross for.

The older I get, the shorter the list of things for which I would cross the I-beam is. I have 16 governing values. But I would cross that I-beam – I would take that risk – for only three things: God, Jesus Christ, and my family. Nothing else. I would risk the walk on the I-beam for those relationships and not for any amount of money, fancy plaques or titles.

If you understand your values, your inner self, you have unleashed a driving force in your own personal path to form a purposeful retirement. You know what you value, and therefore you know where you should direct your time, your energy, and your resources.

A Clarifying Statement

To help solidify these governing values, it helps to write a clarifying statement for each governing value and describe exactly what each value means to you.

For example, in going through this process with a seminar participant, she explained that a governing value in her life was good health. Her clarifying statement looked like this:

Good Health

I walk five days a week.

I find and try one new, healthy recipe a month.

I make choices to bring more laughter into my life.

Another participant identified the personal governing value of Growing Intellectually. Her clarifying statement read:

I Grow Intellectually

I take the time to read two good books a month, one fiction and one nonfiction. I seek opportunities within my community to help me grow. I choose to take classes to expand my knowledge into other areas.

Prioritizing Your Governing Values

The last step in forming a personal constitution is to prioritize your governing values, those things in your life you would cross the I-beam for, in order of importance. You may value love, honesty, loyalty, good health, and education. But in what order? You only have 24 hours. Those hours can be purposeful and productive—not mindlessly busy—once we understand what matters most.

These three steps—identify, clarify, and prioritize—illuminate your priorities. Now the challenge is to build a retirement that reflects these values. Once you have identified who you are through the process of developing a personal constitution, you will absolutely know what you want to do in this season of your life.

You're retired. You no longer have to punch a time clock. What you do with your time is yours to dictate. If you want to make a difference in your family, your neighborhood, your church, your community, you have the ability to take needed steps to ensure that your time is spent doing what matters and what reflects your personal constitution.

Purposeful Planning Questions:

1. Put yourself on the I-Beam above the Grand Canyon. Who or what would you cross the I-Beam for?

2. Does your management of time reflect your governing values?

3. Are you giving the most time to that which matters most?

4. What can you do tomorrow to ensure your time aligns with your priorities?

Chapter 4

Purposeful Planning

Now that you understand who you are and what you want to do, let's begin to make a plan.

The benefit of having a plan for a purposeful retirement is that you are able to consciously choose those things that have value and then you are able to spend our retirement acting on those things which you value. You aren't drifting or, busily doing a whole lot of nothing. The need for planning does not stop when you retire. You just have more time to play with; you just have more time within your control. What do you want to do with it?

Before you speak, listen.
Before you write, think.
Before you spend, earn.
Before you invest, investigate.
Before you criticize, wait.
Before you pray, forgive.
Before you quit, try.
Before you retire, save.
Before you die, give.

– William A. Ward

Blowing Up Europe

Let me tell you a story about the importance of planning. It happened when I almost blew up a part of Europe. It was 1968, a really tense time.

Czechoslovakia had recently been invaded, and we were prepared to fire nuclear missiles at a moment's notice. In fact, we were warned to be prepared to launch a missile at any time. For three entire weeks we were actively standing by.

One night in particular, there was an active fire message. Near me, a nuclear missile went erect. Until it didn't.

The missile was supported by a platform which supports the weight of –the missile with three hydraulic legs. This weight is significant. Each missile weighed approximately two tons. This night, while the missile was going up, one of the three legs retracted and the missile started to fall. Painfully. Slowly. But still, falling over. A two ton nuclear missile. Imagine it.

Everyone started to panic. Not only was it a nuclear warhead, but the entire missile itself was two tons. We couldn't exactly reach out and catch it.

There was a back-up. The back-up was a manual crank system. But it would take minutes that we did not have. In all of the chaos, a warrant officer, a veteran of Normandy, studied it carefully for a few seconds. Finally, he walked over to the power station which controlled the system, hit a few buttons, and the leg started to work. The crisis was over!

Stunned, I asked him, "Why didn't you act sooner? What the hell took you so long?"

"I was planning," he said. "I had to plan what needed to be done. I had to create a plan. And once that was done, it was easy."

Just like this veteran, you need a plan.

Your Sequence Of Events

We all live in what can be called "The Age of Timelock." Because modern conveniences give us more 'time', we have created more options to fill that time, including spending more time unproductively. And we expect ourselves to move as quickly as everything around us. We are all caught up on the treadmill of life, with detrimental consequences.

For example, if your great-grandfather missed his stagecoach, what did he do? He might have tried to catch up to it or wait until the next one ventured through. If your grandmother missed her train, what did she do? She probably waited for the next one. If my father missed an airplane, he probably asked for help to get a seat on the next one. If you and I are temporarily stopped by a red light, we curse the traffic gods as we wait the two minutes for the light to turn green again. What has happened to us? We're timelocked.

Ralph Keyes wrote a book called *We can't be Given More Time* where he compared gridlock to our use of time.

> "Timelock is the condition that occurs when claims on our time have grown so demanding that we feel it's impossible to wring one more second out of a crowded calendar." -**Keyes.**

Retirement is the perfect time to break free of this timelock.

I am a time management expert. I have written many books and put out many products to help people make the best use of their time. I have learned that nearly everyone assumes time management has something to do with the clock.

The clock tells you nothing about time. Time is the occurrence of events in sequence one after the other. If that is true, the only things I can control about time are the events in my life.

> *"Retirement is wonderful. It's doing nothing without worrying about getting caught at it."*
>
> **– Gene Perret**

- I can control when I get out of bed.

- I can control whether or not I want to go swimming before lunch.

- I can control when I have dinner and who I choose to have dinner with.

The awareness of this control is critical because time management is about making choices.

When someone says, "I'm sorry, I do not have time for. . ." that is not true. We all have 24 hours. Just 24 hours. I have the same amount of time that you have, that Warren Buffet has – even Bill Gates has: 24 hours. So if you catch me saying, "I'm sorry, I do not have time for. . ." I am actually saying that I value something more. I am making a choice and choosing the sequence of events in my day.

Think about the Super Bowl or the World Series. It's amazing how many very busy people can put everything on hold to host or attend a Super Bowl party or watch the World Series. It shows what we value. If something matters to us, we find time for it, period.

If I say, "I do not have time to talk today," I am actually saying, "I want to do some other thing even more. I would rather do something else because I value something else more."

On the other hand, if I spend time with you, I am absolutely expressing that you have value to me because I make time for what I value.

So do you! You make time for what you value.

The question now is: what do you value? You have 24 hours. What sequence of events are you choosing to put in your day?

It doesn't matter what you choose to do.

- Read a book.

- Go for a run.

- Have lunch with a friend.

- Play golf with your brother.

- Take a water aerobics class.

There is no hierarchy of choices. What does matter is that you choose to do something.

Choose to do something that will give you a reason to get out of bed in the morning.

Choose to do something that will put some space between you and the recliner.

Choose to do something that will give purpose to your retirement.

Choose to live a purposeful retirement.

When Kareen Knight retired from her job at a nuclear laboratory, she knew she wanted to do something meaningful.

"I looked at several options. I considered Court Appointed Special Advocates (CASA), Retired & Service Volunteer Program (RSVP), and I know people who have volunteered their time through the nationwide Foster Grandparent program. There really are so many options."

But Kareen knew she did not need to be a "foster" grandparent. Her own grandchildren were in elementary school, and she thought they might need some help.

"It was a good fit for me," she said. "And I stayed there until all three grandsons were out of the school. Then I moved to a different grandson's elementary school. I liked the teacher and I have been working with her for the last 20 years."

Kareen volunteers twice a week. She does not have a background in education. But she likes kids, and that's all that is required.

"It is something easy; anyone can do it," she said. "You just have to be reliable. And you have to like kids. I happen to like little kids much more than teenagers or even most adults."

Kareen believes a third to a half of all the students she works with are minority students struggling to speak — let alone read— English, and many of the students come from poverty-income-level homes.

"Some of their home situations are really sad," Kareen said. "Technically, I help with reading. But lately I feel my job has changed. It's my responsibility to get to know these kids, know their names, express interest in them, give them hugs. They need to know someone cares about them. I think that's 90 percent of my job now." Now that her own grandchildren have moved on, she does have time to be that "foster" grandparent.

The Hope of Making A Difference

I've shared this story in previous books, but I believe it's important to share here as well. Many, many years ago when I was volunteering two years of my life for my church, I had the opportunity to hear Winston Churchill speak.

My high school teacher recognized Winston Churchill as a hero of the 20th Century. He taught me about Churchill's crucial role in stopping Hitler and how Churchill was a great man in the right place at the right time. And now, basically just a few months later, here I was at Churchill's feet listening to him speak.

"We make a living by what we get, but we make a life by what we give."
–Winston Churchill

It was a speech he gave shortly before his death, and he said that he had been obsessed with the need to make a difference on the planet. I remember him saying that he hoped he had made a difference on the planet.

I couldn't believe what I was hearing! Before I heard him speak, I already acknowledged Churchill as one of the truly great heroes of my time. And here he was, saying that he, Churchill, hoped he had made a difference on the planet. I was shocked! Churchill had saved the free world. If anyone had made a difference, he had. But toward the end of his life and his career, he was still worried about it! He still wanted to be sure he had made a difference. His obsession had not abated.

I decided right then and there that I also wanted to make a difference. And since that day, I periodically stop and ask myself, "Have I made a difference?" At this time in my life, I may not clock in a 40 hour work week, but I'm devoting 40+ years to my new "work."

We need more people willing to make a difference. Sometimes the call to make a difference goes unanswered because people think they are too old or have done enough during their lifetime. "It's time for the next generation to step up and do something!"

The minute you start thinking that you are too old to make a difference in the world, you'll die. The minute you stop making a difference, there is no reason to live, there is only time to die.

I am consciously and wholeheartedly dedicated to making a difference whether it be in my spouse's life, my family, or my community. And this is how I will live until I die.

"Have I made a difference?" Are you ready to take on that question?

Purposeful Planning Questions:

1. Where did you spend your time yesterday?

1. Are you giving your time to what you value?

2. How do you answer this question: Have I made a difference?

3. What can you do tomorrow to help you say "Yes!" to that question?

Chapter 5

Mentoring & Being Mentored

Look around you. We have relatively few examples of how to retire and even fewer examples of how to retire well. Can you think of someone you would like to emulate in retirement? Someone who can mentor you.

Quite a lot has been said about the role retirees can play as mentors. Have you considered the fact that you need a mentor in your own retirement? Just because you are around the age of 65 does not mean there are not some older people around you who can teach you how to retire and retire well!

Take the challenge. Look around and find someone you admire, someone 10–15 years older than you are. Ask them about their retirement.

- How is it going?

- What do you like about your retirement?

- What do you recommend doing?

- What do you wish you had done differently in your retirement, right from the start?

Hopefully they can tell you, "Hey, I've had several fabulous years! Here's how and why."

Lose Yourself

Sometimes you're lucky enough to find those mentors in your own family. My friend, retired professor Steven Baugh, has been consistently mentored by his father through each stage of his life, even retirement. "My father has always been an example to me," he said. "He and my mother are 96 and still living in their own home. We still golf once a week."

As soon as his father retired, he began volunteering. He chose to serve people through AARP and also through opportunities provided by his church.

"Service is innate in everything my father does," he said. "It helps him stay physically active. He never stops. He just keeps going."

Steven has embraced this example. His last official title before retirement was the superintendent of a school district. As you might expect, this high stress position led to him choosing an early retirement. But when he retired at 55, he decided he was not done. He became an Associate Professor and taught for another 14 years.

"When I decided to retire, I was determined to still make a contribution," he said. "My personality demands that I do things. I want to continue to learn.

I want to study and read and make a contribution, because when I'm up and doing things, I'm happy."

"When our day jobs are gone, for our own mental and physical health, we need to find something meaningful to do," he shared with me. "We need to replace that time we spent at work with something else. We need something else to give our attention to and dedicate our time toward."

For Steven, it's his family, his religion, and himself. "My family comes first. Retirement means that I have time for my spouse, children, grandchildren, and even my elderly parents. Second, there's my religion. I have more time for church service, and church service does not need to be something I am assigned to do. There are opportunities for Christian service everywhere. We can get to work without being asked, without being assigned a specific task. Third, I can give service to my own self. I can take care of myself. I can ride my bike. I can play tennis. This activity brings an inner satisfaction. In a way, it replaces and goes a long way toward helping us all make the adjustment from our paid jobs with our fancy titles."

The key, he said, is to lose yourself, to forget yourself. Steven says his father's service and his own service keeps them both happy and alive.

"It is so important to be active in serving others for one's mental, emotional, and spiritual health and well-being," he said. "Losing yourself in doing for others has a very natural byproduct of making you happy and healthy. Not just physically but mentally and spiritually as well."

What Not To Do

We can also be shown how **not** to retire.

Bob Ulin is a good friend, a retired US Army colonel, who is an expert at how to retire well, even though he still has not completely retired. I'll refer to him hereafter as my non-practicing expert. He told me he is modeling his quasi-retirement after two of his mentors in the military.

"One was a former battalion commander," he explained. "This gentleman gave his life to the military and served in many crucial areas and positions. He impacted the way I thought about my own career and the paths I chose for myself. After 38 years of service, now a full colonel, he was told to retire. He didn't want to go. The military was his life. He felt as though he was being kicked out, and he died six months later."

Bob learned one final lesson from this mentor. "I learned that the army is great, but there is more to life after the army. You cannot be so inflexible that what you do in your career is your only passion.

Because when that's gone, you'll just die. You have to be more resilient than that. You have to be willing to adapt in order to stay happy in retirement."

Bob's second mentor was a lieutenant colonel. When he was asked to transfer to a new location, he said he did not want to go. "So he was sent his retirement orders," Bob shared. "The day came for him to retire. On Friday we had a big celebration to wish him well in his retirement. But on Monday morning he showed right back up at the office."

> *"It's paradoxical that the idea of living a long life appeals to everyone, but the idea of getting old doesn't appeal to anyone."*
> **– Andy Rooney**

Bob asked him what he was doing at work. "He said, 'Oh, I just have some things to do.' And I told him, 'No, you don't. You don't work here anymore.' It was confusing for him because his job was all he wanted to do, and he had a really tough time adjusting." Bob made a promise to himself that he would not be like that. "I would not show up back to my old job on Monday morning. I will find something. I will stay stimulated. I will have a fulfilling life. I will be fulfilled by something that has absolutely nothing to do with my past chosen career."

"Each time I try to fully retire, I get pulled right back into a new opportunity, a new reason to get up in the morning. Sometimes I even get paid, which my wife thinks is great," he explained. Bob is not working full-time, though he's certainly had offers. "No, I do not want to do that anymore," he said. "I like sleeping late. I like reading the newspaper and having lunch with my wife. I like being the master of my own schedule."

But since he feels driven to do **something,** Bob has started a nonprofit that helps members of the military transition to the private sector. "As both retired military and a retired business executive, I understand both careers. I have some insight to contribute, not to mention the example of my own personal experience, on how to make an effective transition."

This effort has brought great purpose to Bob's retirement. "I'm doing work that I feel adds value to my own life and to my community. I am keeping my mind mentally active. I need to be in charge of something. I need to see accomplishments. If I am not seeing that, I am not satisfied. Yes, my pace of life has slowed down, but my ability to accomplish things that matter and make a difference has not. I still have great satisfaction by seeing things get accomplished."

Bob's advice for new retirees is simple: "Now that you are retired, you better find out who you are and what you want to do. You better find out what matters to you outside of your day job. And you better get to work doing it."

A Happy Medium

We all know people who retired and then never left their living room again. They go from spending all their time at work to all their time on the couch without a happy medium in the middle.

This is the danger of retiring without a plan, without a purpose, without a motivation to make a difference. Simply because we reach a magical number does not mean we need to turn off our interests, hobbies, passions, or commitment to service.

Picture what you want. Say in your mind or even out loud: "I want my retirement to look like this. . ."

Gather some magazines together on the dining room table and cut out pictures that represent your idea of a great, purposeful retirement. Take your pictures and make a collage.

If you are more comfortable working through computer images, do a Google image search using the term 'perfect retirement.' What comes up? What images speak to you? Save them or copy them into a document and print them off.

What images are you choosing? What does your retirement look like? Who is in it? What are you doing in your picture? What do you want this next season of life to look like?

Now you know what you want it to look like. Now you need to get to work and get there.

Purposeful Planning Questions:

1. Do you have a mentor for your retirement? Make an appointment to take your mentor to lunch and tell them your plan.

2. What does your perfect retirement collage look like?

3. What can you do today to start living a 'perfect' or ideal retirement?

Chapter 6

Make A Difference

You've examined your Belief Window, defined your governing values, and written your personal constitution. You've thought about the importance of utilizing your time with purpose and choosing to have a purposeful, successful retirement as you define it. You are ready to prioritize your life around what matters most in order to make a difference. What next?

Now is the best part. Now you consider your options and move forward to make great ideas turn into a great retirement. Now is the time to act.

Three basic emotions motivate us to act. These three emotions are hierarchal in nature, and no matter what, we function at these levels. The emotions are:

- Fear

- Duty

- Love

Fear is the lowest emotion. With fear, we act because we *have to*. Chances are we've all experienced this throughout our lives.

"I *have to* go to school because if I don't there will be problems at home. . ."

"I *have to* go to work because if I don't there will be no money to . . ."

"I *have to* take my spouse out to dinner because if I don't there will be problems in my marriage. . ."

Fear is a great, strong motivator.

At the next level, we are motivated to act out of duty. With duty, we act because we *ought to*. Again, chances are you've experienced this.

"I *ought to* go to school because it's the right thing to do. . ."

"I *ought to* go to work because it's the right thing to do. . ."

"I *ought to* have a movie night with my partner because it's the right thing to do. . ."

Love is the highest motivator. When we act out of love, we act because we *love to* and are excited to. It's a passion for us.

"I *love to* go to school because it is fun and fulfilling. . ."

"I *love to* go to work because it is fun and fulfilling. . ."

"I *love to* spend time with my spouse because it's fun and fulfilling. . ."

On any given day and any given task, we act through all three emotions. We may make the bed because we fear a spouse's reaction if we don't. We may babysit because we feel a duty, we feel we ought to do so. We may travel with our spouse because we love to do so.

Now, this is your retirement. Set aside the fear and duty. Plan to do what you love to do. When we act out of love, miracles happen. What do you love to do? If you don't know, if you cannot figure it out, the consequences are severe. You'll do nothing. You'll sit, you'll be depressed, and you'll wait to die.

When I started a new job, I used to say, "I'll be here as long as it's fun. When it's no longer fun, I'm out." I think some people have the same approach to life. "I'll be here as long as it's fun. When it's no longer fun, I'm out."

What is fun to you? I'm not talking about a state of constant amusement.

When flood waters hit our community last year, I spent the day digging mud out of a neighbors' basement. But I was making a difference, and that was great to me. Looking back, that day was fun.

What do you want to do?

"There are many good people out there," a friend told me some time ago. "I am continually amazed by how giving people are, how willing they are to help others." But this friend is not as complimentary of people his own age. He is frustrated by how many retirees are satisfied at giving advice and refusing to do much else.

"The days of standing back and watching others work while you watch and 'manage' it all are long past. Retired people need to pull their own weight. Put in the time, energy, and money enough to be part of the solution, not just commentators on the problem.

"We have too many commentators and not enough doers," he said. "Many retirees are fond of talking and reveling in the past about what they did. Don't be stuck in the past. Your stories are interesting, but they do not add value like getting to work and helping. I see retired people who have accomplished great things in their life. They have been good – they've even been lucky – and they have great experience. But then they rest on their laurels and think that they can just sit back and give advice. They have forgotten that they can add value beyond just talking."

Imagine going into a library where nothing is new. In fact, all of the books in this imaginary library are from 1890 or earlier. Now, if that meets with your personal preference, you might think that this is great. As for me, I like to study new things as much as I like to tinker with old. If I walked into such a library, I probably would not stay very long.

You do not have to only pick from old stories. You do not need to rely on previous accomplishments. You can spin new stories. You can write new tales. You're not dead yet!

So do something, especially something new. If you can only talk about what you did in your life, in your job it means that you are not doing anything new; you're not living.

> "I have retired, unretired, and retired again all in the past 10 years. I find the biggest trouble with having NOTHING to do is . . . you can't tell when you are done"
>
> *– Author Unknown.*

Un-Retire

Many people completely fail at retirement. So they go back to work or pursue a new career. You can choose to do the same. I am not talking about going from Adobe to Google. This time, work is about pursuing a passion. This time, work is about doing something you love to do. Ask yourself some probing questions:

- What do you feel passionate about doing?

- What brings you joy?

- Besides getting paid, what did you like about your day job?

- What skills, talents, and business contacts can you take with you?

Remember what you loved most about your last day job and find a way to make it fit into your new life.

After retirement, a friend, Juliann Andreen, packed her bags and moved from Washington, D.C. to San Diego, California. The change of weather inspired her to move and, it made her retirement feel like a permanent vacation.

"San Diego offers a lifestyle different from Washington, D.C.," she said. "And it felt like a vacation all the time. I do not have to rush out and 'enjoy the weather' because guess what, it's going to be the exact same weather tomorrow! It's amazing."

"I love having the additional freedom of time. I love that there are options that I can choose from as I plan out my day. Because it's my choice, my time. But I decided, right from the beginning of my retirement, that I was not going to get lazy, sleep in, and do nothing. I was not going to waste away the hours rocking on my front porch. I get up early, every day, and I make a plan for my day. And guess what? If it doesn't get done that day, there is always tomorrow. I get to decide what I need to do when I want to do it, and that is nice. I am motivated to do certain things but I also have the power to say 'no' to things. That freedom is great!"

But once that wore off a bit, she looked around and realized that she felt a little isolated.

"I have family in San Diego," she said. "And that helped. I am able to check in with my son about once a week, and I enjoy hanging out with my family." But she realized she needed something to do the other six days a week.

"When I first stopped working, I had a list of a million things I wanted to do. And I've done some of those things." But she quickly realized she wanted something more.

So she went back to work, just not in an office and definitely not 40 hours a week. She bought a new property and turned a portion of it into a bed and breakfast. She listed this property on Airbnb.com and has found great success. Her new business adds supplemental income, a focus for her retirement, and a source of entertainment as well, since the Airbnb unit is attached to her own home and she is able to interact with families from all over the world.

"I thought I would miss getting up and going to work every morning," she said. "But I don't. I really don't. Who wants to do that every day again? I missed the friendships and the interaction with people at work and this helps. It is a whole new adventure. And now

I think, 'how did I ever have enough time to go to a real job? I am too busy!' There is always something to be done. There's always a new project! It has made a difference to me, and it is so much fun."

My friend Richard Dubois hated retirement the first time around. So he went back to work. After he retired a second time, he knew he needed to fill his day in a purposeful manner. He chose two things: volunteer work and starting his own real estate business.

"I needed to find something meaningful, something of great interest to me. And real estate is stimulating to me. It is not about the money; it is about helping people make the right decision, at the right time. I see a buyer as an investor. A house is more than warmth, comfort, and shelter. It's really an investment. I enjoy helping people find the right home for the right reason. And I can work as little or as much as I want."

Richard also serves as the Council Commissioner of the Utah National Parks Council of the Boy Scouts of America.

Richard goes on to say, "There are so many places to volunteer. It really is unlimited as long as you feel you are making a difference with people," he said. "I understand people who feel fear and anxiety over new things. But there is only one way to beat that fear: full immersion. If you fully immerse yourself in something new that new project or new technology or new activity you'll find your way. If you just stick your toe in, you will not enjoy it or be successful. And you'll give up."

Volunteer

Are you ready to volunteer? It's easy!

- Find a local community theater and volunteer as an usher.

- Provide rides to the hospital or to the grocery store to someone in need.

- Mentor a child at a local school or through your local library.

- Serve meals at a homeless shelter.

- Play music or sing at a retirement home.

- Mow your neighbor's lawn.

- Teach classes at a community center.

- Repair someone's car.

The "what" does not matter. Look around and find a way to help and volunteer. Find a way to make a difference. We are happiest when we serve.

I am the Vice-Chairman of the Board of Directors for the Tuacahn Center for the Arts[1]. We have over 300 volunteers, and 30-40 of them work every night. They get to see a wonderful show for free. They get to wear an elegant little volunteer vest. They get to make sure that things function smoothly.

We could not function without them. Tuacahn gets the benefit of their service, and they are able to do something that matters. They are serving people, helping them to find their seat and the bathrooms. They are not financially reimbursed, but you could not beat those people away with a stick. They love it. And through their service, they have formed lasting friendships, even outside of the theater. They hang out with each other. They are happy because they are busy and active. They are happy because they know they are needed.

"There is a fountain of youth: it is your mind, your talents, the creativity you bring to your life and the lives of people you love. When you learn to tap this source, you will truly have defeated age."

– Sophia Loren

---

1   www.tuacahn.org

Develop Talents

What did you leave behind in your childhood in order to be a more responsible adult?

- Were you too busy to practice the piano?

- Did your easel and art supplies collect dust or dry up in the back of the closet?

- Did you put your bike into rental storage with just happy memories of riding for miles?

Well, tune the piano. Set up the easel. Get the bike back out of storage.

And now is a great time to go back to school and finish that degree you always wanted. You have the gift of time. Why not use it to the fullest? Why not do it now?

Now your time is yours. You've been a responsible adult your whole life. So what do you want to do now? Go back and get that degree in philosophy if it's what you always wanted to do. Stop watching Top Chef on television and start taking culinary classes. Go to a local guitar shop and sign up for classes. If you don't want to do it alone, take a grandchild. Be the cool grandparent that is always trying new things.

Or you can write. Look at me! Look at the number of books I have written since I "retired." Or you can take up photography. You can travel and act as a tour guide. Or you can do a combination of all of the above.

The important thing is to choose what makes you feel joy and satisfaction, what makes you feel like you are making a difference, and what will help you be happy in your retirement.

Or you can do nothing and just die.

Really, I've seen this. I had a friend who retired and was falling apart. Months after his retirement, he looked like he was ready to die. So I asked him to come out and help me at my ranch.

"I have some vehicles at the ranch I need maintained," I said. "Do you think you have the time to help me?"

He had a great talent for fixing things. While he worked on my ranch, utilizing his talents, he came back to life. He worked for me for several years, showing up with his tools and getting to work. He knew that he mattered. Once again, he felt valued.

He was making a difference. He was living a purposeful retirement.

Learn

When I was young, my father had us memorize a short quote:

You cannot think any deeper than your vocabulary will allow you to.

This is a profound statement. If you want to keep your brain thriving, if you want to keep thinking in a very real manner, you have to keep building your vocabulary. You have to keep learning.

How do you build your vocabulary? How do you keep learning? You read. Or you listen to an audiobook. And you share what you're learning with those around you.

Do you want to hear something scary? Listen to the conversations around you. Go to a shopping mall and listen in on a conversation. Count how many times you hear the word "like".

The word "like" is a filler word used because our youth are lacking any other words to help them express themselves. They have a limited vocabulary. But do not get on your "This Generation!" high horse. We need to stop talking about this generation as though we had nothing to do with creating it. We need to stop judging and start modeling better behavior. And we need to start with ourselves.

You do not have to go back to school or spend any time in a classroom, but that is certainly an option. Many local colleges offer continuing education opportunities. They are wonderful opportunities because they provide structure to the learning process. And it gives you some place to go!

If you do not want to go to a class or return to formal education, choose to learn outside of the classroom.

- Study great literature.

- Form a book club.

- Learn a new word every week.

- Learn to cook.

- Learn to play a musical instrument.

- Learn a new language.

- Study local history and visit the places you learn about.

- Research your own family history.

- Go to an assisted-living facility, find someone even older than you, and read to them.

Whatever you choose to do, make it a priority. Take care of your brain. Go to an art museum and read the pamphlet on the artist. Read the book before you watch the movie. If you want to travel internationally, spend some time learning some foreign language basics. Keep your brain sharp and active.

My non-practicing expert at retiring, Bob Ulin, tries to learn something new every day. "I have three books going at a time," he told me. He calls this his "habit of learning." He takes classes on subjects he wants to learn or refresher courses for subjects in which he has a strong background.

"It is healthy to be a lifelong learner," Bob said. "I love history; I love to read history. I have over 800 books in my library." He's officially out of shelf space, and even his e-reader is getting a little full. Continually learning gives him a sense of great fulfillment; he is doing something that matters when he increases his own knowledge. Bob has co-authored two books on European security policy, published his memoir, and written a how-to book entitled *Transitions*.

"Find what you want to do," is his suggestion to other retirees. "Find what you are comfortable doing, because doing nothing should never be an option."

"I have a friend who works on his farm," he also shared. "He is a bright man, a West Point graduate. Now that he is retired, he mucks out stalls and takes great care of his horses. He clears brush on his land and on his acreage. He gets fulfillment from that.

"Retirement may be looked upon either as a
prolonged holiday or as a rejection,
a being thrown on to the scrap-heap."
– Simone de Beauvoir

But that is not for me. Everyone needs to find what they are personally good at. They need to look for new ways to stay physically and intellectually active."

You can learn new things in your retirement away from a book or even a computer course. Any new experience can be a learning experience. The important thing is to stay mentally active. When you are mentally active, you are learning.

My wife, Gail, is a wonderful example to me as she continues to learn and use technology in various projects. Even though she realizes the grandkids can do something ten times faster, Gail never gets intimidated by new technology and never gives up. "When things are a challenge, I like to take them on," she explains. "I just hit it, head-on. I don't let myself be afraid."

My friend that refuses to fully retire, Arlen Crouch, makes it a point to take time to text his grandkids often. He refuses to be scared of new technology or new gadgets.

"The technology available to us today is so different than 20 years ago. But don't ignore it."

Do you have the bad habit of calling for help whenever you log in to the internet? Stop it. "Learn how to work your computer," Arlen says. "Find out how to post something on Facebook. And do it today. The older you get, the further away it gets, and you need to understand how to communicate today."

Arlen does not just preach. He is one of the first people in line to figure out a new skill. He understood he did not know how to work the computer software Excel. So he took a class.

"A lot of times when you retire, you stop growing. You stop learning. I don't want to do that. I reached a point where I realized working Excel was hard. I had to admit to myself, 'Man, this is over my head.' So I took a class. I practiced. Now I can do it just as well as anybody can. You have to refuse to be afraid of technology, and learn what you can."

Leave A Legacy

I met Ann Barnes a few chapters ago. If Ann had not been diagnosed with cancer, she probably would still be in a classroom somewhere. She spent the early part of her career teaching K-12, but toward the end of her career, she was teaching education at the university level.

"I failed at retirement," she admits. "My husband was also a professor, and we were not ready to quit. We liked the challenge. We liked doing different things every day."

They decided to return to teaching. Ann moved with her husband to Hawaii, where she taught at BYU Hawaii and her husband taught at the University of Hawaii.

"We were doing exactly what we wanted to do. We were ready and excited to embark on a new adventure."

But life handed Ann a new plan, and she was diagnosed with cancer. To more aggressively fight the cancer, Ann chose to leave her job and even her home in Hawaii. "We made a decision to move to Utah to be closer to the Huntsman Cancer Institute at the University of Utah because of my little run-in with cancer."

Ann's retirement was not her own decision. It was not on purpose, and it was certainly not purposeful. "But life intervened and we responded," she said.

"It was during that time when I was alone a lot that I made a decision. I had time to think. And I decided that if I got another season in life, I wanted to do what I really wanted to do. It was actually a great blessing, because most people do not have the time and energy to consider their retirement that way, to ask themselves, 'What is it that I really want to leave as my legacy?'"

> "You don't stop laughing when you grow old, you grow old when you stop laughing."
> **−George Bernard Shaw**

Ann decided her grandkids were going to be her legacy. And if she was not going to be around for them, she wanted to make sure that they had each other. "We wanted to leave our grandchildren a legacy, not of money but of each other. We wanted to create a 16-person gang. A good kind of gang. So that even after we were not around anymore, they would have each other."

Ann created "Cousin Camp." It's a week every year where all the grandkids come, without their parents, and build relationships with each other. They play together. They serve together, whether it's turning scrap lumber into toys for a local charity or going door-to-door to collect food for a food bank.

"Our neighbors look at it and think we are giving our kids a break by taking the grandkids for a week. They see us doing this out of concern for our kids," Ann said. "That is an unintended outcome. It is a byproduct. But it's not why we do it. We even discourage our kids from thinking of it that way, because it reframes it in a way that we do not intend. It's about the kids. It's about their relationship together. We just finished our tenth Cousin Camp and it is hard to overstate how important it has been to our happiness and our sense of purpose about who we are."

It's not a cheap endeavor. "Cousin Camp started off with just our 4-7 year olds. They are bigger now, and they eat more!" Ann laughs. "And driving to the park and running through the sprinklers will not cut it anymore as an activity! It's an investment of time, money, everything. But it's worth it. It's worth all of it."

Cousin Camp is the flagship. "But it's not the only thing we do," Ann says. "The kids use social media. They FaceTime with each other all the time. They are states apart but 100 percent connected to each other. They have an ongoing text chat-stream where they talk all the time. It is hugely gratifying to see those relationships."

"A lot of grandparents want to spend time with their grandkids because they love them and want to express that love and create memories. We do that, too. We love that one-on-one time. That's great. We want that, too. But we also wanted to create a gang devoted to each other and help them develop commitments to each other."

Ann saw her fight with cancer as a gift. It helped her stop and prioritize and make the time to make a difference.

"My daughter-in-law told me the other day that the cousins were not really cousins, they were extended siblings," Ann shared. "Right when she said that, I realized, 'Wow, we did it!' We struck gold. We have developed exactly what we wanted for ourselves and them."

While waiting for my first appointment in the reception room of a new dentist, I noticed his certificate hanging on the wall; it gave his full name. Thinking hard, I remembered that a tall, handsome boy with the same name had been in my high school class some 36 years ago.

Upon seeing him, however, I quickly discarded any such thought. This balding, grey-haired man with the deeply lined face was way too old to have been my classmate.

After he had examined my teeth, I asked him if he had attended the local high school.

'Yes,' he replied.

'When did you graduate?' I asked.

He answered, 'In 1971. Why?'

'You were in my class!' I exclaimed.

He looked at me closely, and then the thoughtless idiot asked, 'What did you teach?'

Explore

In our friends' home hangs a world map and that map is covered with a multitude of little white pins. Our friends have pinned everywhere in the world they have visited. It helps them plan their next adventure. Where should we go next? Well, what area of the map is pinless?

"We would like to go everywhere we can on the planet. There is not a single place that does not sound cool," my friend explained. This sense of adventure seems to have skipped a generation, however. Each and every new adventure seems to scare their kids in an odd role reversal. "When we were planning our trip to Egypt right after the riots, it drove our kids crazy!" my friend shared. "Our son asked us, 'Where are you going next? Afghanistan?' Without missing a beat, my husband looked at me and calmly said, 'You know, I bet we could get some real good deals on travel there right now.'"

"We are not super crazy. But we refuse to be held down by fear. We figure out where we want to go, what we want to see, and then we do it. But it's not for everyone. I saw my cousin at a family wedding and asked him how his retirement is going. 'It's great!' he said. When I asked him what was great, he said, 'Our dream was to live on a lake and fish every day. We made it happen. We moved from the city to the country. We fish every day. It is our dream come true. I am living my dream every day.'"

Everyone has their own dream retirement. The difficulty is being brave enough to make that dream come true, whether it's fishing every day or seeing the world.

Many retirees seem to choose the last option. They want to see the pyramids in Egypt and not just on a movie they are watching with their grandkids! When it comes to exploring the world, cruises are a popular retirement option. Have you considered the fact that a cruise is essentially a rest home in boat form or a rest home on steroids? Have you considered the similarities? Your food is provided for you, there is scheduled entertainment, someone makes your bed and helps you throughout your activities. Like I said, a rest home on steroids. Don't get me wrong, I love it and its a great way to see the world.

I realized this when my wife and I went to explore the Greek Islands. We were joined on the cruise by 1,800 other people. At dinner I had an opportunity to really take a closer look at our shipmates.

"Gail," I whispered, leaning across our table. "What are we doing? We're on a boat with a bunch of old people!"

"Hyrum," she whispered back. "Have you looked in the mirror? **These are your people**!"

I have a friend who is a veteran and is absolutely done with traveling. I have explained that Europe looks a lot better now than it did after the last World War, but he is slow to be convinced. He is firmly committed to the joy of the staycation.

"I do not like to travel," he explained to me. "I have lived abroad for 20 years. That's enough. Now I just want to spend time with my wife and enjoy the fruit of what we have built together."

So he has created the ultimate staycation. He landscaped and improved his backyard to the point where he had created his very own vacation stop.

"We look at the yard, and we are fulfilled everyday as we have breakfast on the back deck. We have been in some exotic and some nasty places while serving in the military. It is not thrilling anymore. We would rather stay here, eat good food, enjoy our wine cellar, and entertain friends."

Be Fully Present

Did you retire from a high stress job? Did you come home engulfed in clouds of stress as you struggled to leave the office at the office?

Through retirement, you can decide to be fully present. You no longer have to straddle two separate worlds.

As I mentioned earlier, my friend, retired professor Steven Baugh, had worked as a school district superintendent.

"I was responsible for 45,000 students," he said. "I had 5,000 employees. I oversaw a $200 million budget. It was extremely demanding. I tried to leave the stress of work at work and when I wanted to be home and fully present with my family when I came home. But I guess I was really bad at it. My wife commented after my first retirement that is was so nice to have me 'really be home and relaxed.' It was a wake-up call for me. I did not realize that I was bringing the stress home with me. A benefit of retirement was that I got to leave that all behind."

"I enjoy waking up and not having to go to work. So I do it three or four times a day."
– Gene Perret

He left the bad and he chose to move forward with the good by being fully present at home with his family. We can all do the same.

When you are fully present with someone, it means you are intently listening and hearing what they have to say to you. When I was working full-time and had an appointment with an employee, I would close the door, take the phone off of the hook, and ask my assistant to prevent all interruptions. I was focused on them and what we needed to accomplish during our time together. During our meeting, whoever I was talking to knew they had my full attention and nothing would interrupt us. I maintained eye contact. I did not look away, read emails, or quickly check my phone. I was fully present.

In retirement, I keep that commitment to being fully present to the people around me. When my grandkids enter my home, they know they need to put all devices in a basket by the door. And since I keep a hammer by the basket, they take it seriously. It forces my grandkids to interact with us and each other. Otherwise, they'd disappear into their own devices.

I am also a big proponent of making an appointment with your spouse. Sit down with each other. Talk. No cell phones, no iPads, just talking and planning together on a regular, scheduled basis. Be present with each other.

Do It

Whatever you want to do, start today and actually do it.

Bucket lists are hugely popular these days. Though nothing is wrong with making a bucket list, I have never pushed them. It's great if you want to write one up. My only comment is this: if you have one, make it doable.

While I have not set my dreams down in the form of a bucket list, I am a big daydreamer. It's how I used to relax, particularly when I was travelling all the time. I would sit in that plane seat, put my mind in neutral, and just daydream. I'd think about what I would do if I was the president of the United States. I would daydream about being a diplomat and traveling to exotic countries. Sometimes I'd even wonder what I would do if I was the king of the entire world for a year. Unlimited power as the absolute monarch of the entire earth for an entire year! What would I do?

> "A man is not old until regrets take the place of dreams."
> *– John Barrymore*

I used to teach a workshop where I would ask participants to write down something they would really like to do if time and money were no object. Here are a few of their responses:

- Build a hope chest for my wife.

- Lock myself in a cabin with enough food and books for a month.

- Learn a new language.

- Audition and be part of a play.

- Travel and eat where all the locals eat.

- Bicycle to the ocean.

- Wake up on my own time without an alarm.

- Fly an airplane.

The responses were as diverse as the people who wrote them. We all have things we want to accomplish, but we've pushed down these desires in order to 'get a real job', or start a family, or just live as the world dictates that we should. We never gave ourselves permission to sit down and say: "What would I really like to do? When am I going to do it?"

You've never given yourself permission, so I'm going to give it to you right now. Go ahead and ask yourself: "What would I really like to do? When am I going to do it?" Go ahead! Write your answers right here in the margins!

"We have friends we tell about our trips," a friend told me, "and they all say that someday they might want to go, too. We hear it all the time! 'I would like to...someday. I might want to try it. . .someday.' Don't they realize we're running out of somedays? It's hard. It takes energy to make trips happen, it takes planning to go on adventures. But go! Go!"

My wife and I recently took a trip to Denver, Colorado. We did not just dream ourselves there. We made a plan.

- Research Denver Attractions

- Get a hotel reservation in Grand Junction so we are not driving too much each day.

- Schedule the dates to go.

- Make arrangements for someone to watch over the ranch while we're gone.

- Fill up the car with gas.

- Pack snacks.

- Check a map.

- Bring money for food.

We had benchmarks along our way, and those benchmarks allowed us to have an actionable plan.

What do you want to do? What benchmarks do you have to get you there? Turn your daydreams into an actionable plan, and do it today!

Purposeful Planning Questions:

1. As you read this chapter, what options stuck out to you?

2. What options discussed in this chapter are you going to act on?

3. What can you do today to act on an option?

Chapter 7

Retiring Together

Many years ago a physician in Japan started seeing some alarming health symptoms in women. His patients were plagued by depression, headaches, stomach ulcers, and even stress-induced rashes.

He realized they were all suffering from the same thing, and he aptly named the physical result the "retired husband syndrome." He thought that as many as 60 percent of wives of Japanese retirees suffered from the same ailment.

This is certainly not a problem only seen in Japan. In America, we seem to be suffering from what is commonly called "Gray Divorce."

Fortune Teller

In a dim, smoky room, the psychic turned the cards up one by one, and told her client the shocking truth:

"There is no gentle way to tell you this, so I'll just say it. Prepare for widowhood. Your husband will die horribly and violently before the year is out."

Noticeably disturbed, the client stared at the old mystic, then at the lone, wavering candle, and finally at the cards laid out before her.

She breathed in deeply, trying to control her emotions. She had to find out the rest. She could not leave without knowing.

She gazed intently at the old woman, prepared herself, and asked, "Is there any chance I'll be acquitted?"

"Gray Divorce" is the name given to the phenomenon of a high divorce rate after retirement. Gone are the days when you only spent a few fleeting hours with your spouse. Now that you are retired, you are with each other day in and day out.

All day in and all day out.

This can be too much for some couples. After retirement, you may look at each other and wonder, "Do I even know who this person is? And do I like this person anymore?"

We are living longer and choosing paths different from our parents. Baby boomers, the generation born between 1946 and 1964, divorce at a rate over three times higher than their parents' generation, and the divorce rate of seniors has doubled in the last twenty years. The U.S. Census reported that the percentage of couples who reach their 20th anniversary has decreased by 20 percent for couples married between 1955 and 1984. Retirement is an emotional time. Your identity is gone. Your predictable schedule is gone. The structure of your time is gone.

Let me share something with you.

You may be really hard to live with during this time.

Bob Ulin, my non-practicing expert at retirement, quickly learned that he needed to keep busy in retirement solely for the purpose of staying out of his wife's way. He watched friends, he said, leave their day job and then get fat and stupid. "I have never allowed that," he said. "I have to do something, preferably something that keeps me out of my wife's hair. When I retired, she told me the problem with retired husbands is that you get twice as much husband but only half as much money. She has a very valid point."

The Ulins have worked together and found a way to "share space," but yet "not breathe down each other's necks. We have time apart and time together, and that allows our time together to be satisfying. I am not going to tell you that everything is always roses. I will tell you that if you are going to make marriage work after retirement, you need to have things you do together and things you do separately."

Preparing To Adjust

The marriage you have before retirement is the marriage you will have after retirement, only amplified. In your retirement, you will reap what you have sown during your partnership. Have you worked together as a team? Or have your paths led away from each other more than they have come together?

- The husband who complained about dinner not being ready when he was working will be the husband who now complains about breakfast, lunch AND dinner.

- The wife who complained about towels on the floor will now complain about dirt from the garden finding its way through the kitchen, the living room, and the dining room.

- The wife who complains about the husband who is never home will turn into the wife who complains that her husband never leaves the couch.

- The husband who received much of his wife's attention when home will be resentful when she leaves during the day for a lunch date with a former colleague.

The issues that exist throughout your marriage will still be there after retirement but may be harder to ignore with an increased level of time together.

How many times have you had to adjust to new situations in your marriage?

- Have you gone from a two-career family down to a one-career family?

- Have you switched jobs to one which required you to travel more?

- Have you had periods of unemployment?

- Have you stopped working to raise a family?

- Have you adjusted to life as your kids went to college and you were left with an empty nest?

The more adjustments you've already overcome, the more successful you may be now.

"I think that the couples who struggle are the couples who have had the same dynamic their entire marriage," a friend explained to me. "This adjustment of retirement will be easier for couples who have maintained separate schedules and juggled multiple things and had to adjust continuously through their marriage."

This friend went on a four month cruise with her spouse. "We shared one little cabin for four months. That's a lot of time together. We handled it really well because through our marriage we have learned how to work well together, and it has translated into our retirement."

An elderly man lay dying in his bed. In death's agony, he suddenly smelled the aroma of his favorite chocolate chip cookies wafting up the stairs. He gathered his remaining strength and lifted himself from the bed.

Leaning against the wall he slowly made his way out of the bedroom, and with even greater effort, forced himself down the stairs, gripping the railing with both hands, and crawled downstairs.

With labored breath, he leaned against the door frame gazing into the kitchen. Were it not for death's agony, he would have thought himself already in heaven. There, spread out upon waxed paper on the kitchen table were literally hundreds of his favorite chocolate chip cookies.

Was it heaven? Or was it one final act of heroic love from his devoted wife, seeing to it that he left this world a happy man? Mustering one great final effort, he threw himself toward the table landing on his knees in a rumpled posture. His parched lips parted; the wondrous taste of the cookie was already in his mouth, seemingly bringing him back to life.

The aged and withered hand trembled on its way to a cookie at the edge of the table when it was suddenly smacked with a spatula by his wife.

"Stay out of those." she said, "They're for the funeral."

An Emotional Playbook

Columnist Miriam Goodman wrote an outline of how to create an Emotional Playbook for new retirees. She wrote: "You wouldn't dream of retiring without a financial game plan, but what so many couples fail to realize is that they also need an emotional playbook. Tremendous conflict can arise when partners fail to articulate their hopes and dreams for retirement, as well as their candid fears about the future."

We briefly met retired Air Force Colonel Kenneth Page a few pages ago. He attacked retirement with an emotional playbook which could have won the

Super Bowl. He credits his plan, as well as his military background, with helping him make a successful transition.

"The Air Force invests a lot of money in training commanders how to treat people – how to lead from the front, not the back," he said. "It's beat into you to always treat people with respect. It made the transition of retirement for my wife and me really quite easy."

He created the following list to help set expectations and ensure that he and Mrs. Page were. . .on the same page.

They got together and discussed the following questions:

- How will household responsibilities change with both spouses at home? Will they be evenly divided?

- Is part-time work an option, part of the plan, or not part of the plan?

- Do either or both spouses want to travel? If so, how often and at what cost?

- What activities do either or both spouses plan to engage in? How will these activities be balanced?

- What activities can you do together to strengthen your relationship?

- What are both spouses' expectations regarding family activities?

- Do you plan to downsize your home, move into a retirement community, move into assisted living, or try to remain in your home forever?

Dividing Chores

Newlyweds are often cautioned to be careful when doing chores after marriage. If you take out the garbage that first day home after the wedding and honeymoon, suddenly that's your job for the rest of your life. If you unload the dishwasher, get ready to do it a million more times over the course of your marriage.

> *"Age is only a number, a cipher for the records.*
> *A man can't retire his experience.*
> *He must use it."*
> **– Bernard Baruch**

Retirement is a similar transition. But now you know better, and when you know better, you do better. Talk about how to divide things so one spouse is not unfairly burdened. If you do not retire at the same time, the spouse who has been home the longest may look forward to help. It's time for a new negotiation.

Have you learned how to successfully negotiate through your marriage? I hope so. In case you can use some tips, there are five steps Gail and I try to live by in negotiating together:

1. Choose a good time to talk. If there is a decision to be made, try not to talk about it in times of stress. Make an appointment and keep the appointment!

2. Give each other your full attention. Remove all distractions. Discuss the decision to be made and lay out the options.

3. Thoroughly discuss all options and perspectives.

4. Never give up and say, "I don't care!" if you care. You'll both end up miserable if you do.

5. Choose a solution that works for both of you.

At the end of your negotiation, both parties must be satisfied or both of you will be miserable. If you reach a good compromise, you will reap the benefits of it.

Colonel Page shared: "My father kept his old chores – mowing the lawn, shoveling the snow. But my mom did everything else, even after my father retired. It was apparent to me that only my dad was able to 'retire.' My mom still had the same amount of work. I often thought, 'where is her retirement?' I realized that when both spouses are retired, husbands need to pick up chores, particularly ones he did not do before."

It's a new beginning. Talk with one another and find a new routine that works for both of you. But as you adjust, remember to have expectations for yourself, but not expectations for your partner. It is no longer your job to establish expectations for someone else. A friend recently told me, "If the bed's not made and it is bothering me, then I make it. It's a way to maintain sanity and happiness. In my retirement, I need to have expectations for myself. But I cannot force them on my partner."

That friend is happily retired and happily married.

Continuing To Work

Though my friend Arlen Crouch, former Merrill Lynch Executive and former CEO at Franklin Quest, has 'retired' from some positions, he still is not fully retired. Sure, he does not work the traditional 40 hour work week. But he works enough to keep his income steady.

"Retirement does not need to change many things. You can find a way to keep busy and stay involved. You can keep income coming in some way," he explained. "It has the added benefit of reducing stress. This time of retirement can be more than taking cruises and playing golf. Keep going. Keep the same interests and add them. Trouble comes when you've allowed yourself to be bored for months on end."

You can choose to work enough to keep you engaged or to help ease any financial concerns. That's your choice, talk about it.

I know a man who retired from his position at a major tech company several years ago, but he decided to keep consulting. He liked remaining slightly engaged and felt better when he knew he had a little bit of income coming in. "It's my beer and poker money," he laughed, because he does not drink and he does not gamble, but 'fly-fishing money' did not sound as interesting. "It's cash that I can have fun with and not have to dip into my retirement."

Traveling Together

We all see bad things on the news. The threat of terrorism may make you consider staying home and staying safe. You don't have to travel. You don't have to go from the conference room of your office straight to the next cruise ship. But maybe your spouse would like to do just that.

Clarify expectations. A friend recently retired. She was newly married; she was married for only five years before she retired. One of the things she liked about her husband was that he was an attorney who had travelled extensively during his career. My friend had taken French in high school and had dreamed for 50 years of going to France. Now she finally had the time to go and a husband who was very familiar with international travel and could make the process very easy. After all, he did it all the time!

Except he didn't want to go. He was done travelling. He was ready to stay home. He told her if she wanted to practice her French perhaps they could take a day trip up to Quebec. My friend was crushed.

Before you retire, there must be pure and honest communication about what you value and what values you want to act on in your retirement. If the goals are dramatically different, there will be problems. In fact, there are a fair number of people choosing divorce over choosing to live under their spouse's ideal retirement plan. Not only is a spouse dismayed that the other one is home all day long, but they cannot agree on what to do. This is a crisis state that never should have deteriorated to this level. Relationships need to be nurtured before retirement so that when you are together all day long, the idea makes you happy, instead of panicked and depressed.

Pursuing Activities

A husband may expect to spend many retirement days quietly fishing, while a spouse may want to dust off their passports and visit new sites. Discuss what may work best for both of you.

"I saw this with my parents," Colonel Page shared. "When my dad retired, he wanted to go camping, hiking, fishing, and he would be gone a lot. My mother played along with it. Not always happily. I watched and realized things could have been done differently."

A friend told me the other day that her mother resented each and every time her dad went fishing or played golf after he retired. "And she let her feelings be known to everyone around her," my friend remembered. So now that my friend is retired, she happily hands off the golf clubs to her husband and even joins him occasionally. "I did not want that animosity in my marriage," she said. "I chose to recognize that we do not all enjoy the same things, and it's good to do things separately. It makes when we come together an even better experience." But look at what she said. It was not a natural feeling to not feel left behind when her husband left or resent his outing without her. It was a choice.

Having Fun Together

Are you meeting up for lunch but spending the mornings apart? You may want to clarify expectations so no one is disappointed or resentful.

My friend who retired from IBM, Richard Dubois, shared with me that, "The beautiful thing about retirement is that you are able to spend more time with your spouse, your children and your grandchildren. But getting used to that extra time is an adjustment. When I was working, I would leave the house at 7 am and come back home for dinner. My facetime with my wife and children was very short. And so, as we were talking about retirement getting closer and what we were going to do to get ready, my wife said, 'I'm not sure I can take you all day long!'"

It may make you laugh, but it is a very real consideration. You have to be willing to make an adjustment.

"You have to foster that relationship," he said. "You have to listen. You have to be patient. You have to allow for quiet time and personal space."

No matter how great your marriage is, there can be such a thing as too much time together. Encourage your spouse to meet up with friends. Send them out on activities and lunches. Do not hold each other back. You'll both be happier for it.

Family Activities

WHEN I'M AN OLD LADY
When I'm an old lady, I'll live with my son,
And make his life happy and filled with such fun,
I want to pay back all the joy he's provided,
Returning each deed. Oh, he'll be so excited. ....

When I'm an old lady and live with my son.
I'll write on the wall with red, white, and blue;
And bounce on the furniture wearing my shoes.
I'll drink from the carton and then leave it out.
I'll stuff all the toilets, and oh, will he shout! .....

When I'm an old lady and live with my son.
When he's on the phone and just out of reach,
I'll get into things like sugar and bleach.
Oh, he'll snap his fingers and then shake his head,
And when he is done I'll hide under the bed. .....

When I'm an old lady and live with my son.
When my son's wife cooks dinner and calls me to meals,
I'll not eat my green beans or salads congealed.
I'll gag on my okra, spill milk on the table,
And when she gets angry, run fast as I'm able. .....

When I'm an old lady and live with my son.
I'll sit close to the TV, thru the channels I'll click,
I'll cross both my eyes to see if they stick,
I'll take off my socks and throw one away,
And play in the mud until the end of the day. .....

When I'm an old lady and live with my son.
And later, in bed, I'll lay back and sigh,
And thank God in prayer and then close my eyes;
And my son will look down with a smile slowly creeping,
And say with a groan, "she's so sweet when she's sleeping,"

When I'm an old lady and live with my son.
–P. Benoit

You may also want to speak with your kids about what they expect in this new stage. You'll have to adjust in your relationship and expectations with your kids want, too. (But, no matter what, take the time to spoil your grandchildren as much as you can!)

Before he retired, my friend Richard and his wife Kathy set their priorities. They decided to focus on their family, serve in their church, and volunteer in their community. "It's great," Richard said. "But we also believe that we need time apart from one another to pursue our own activities. It is important for us to do that. I spend a lot of time in scouting, both at the area and regional level. I spend time with my parents. I ride my bicycle on a local trail four times a week. Kathy has a reading group, and she also bowls with a group of women. While we enjoy spending time together, we realize that we are happier when we pursue other things and then come back to each other."

Living Arrangements

Your spouse may want to sell everything, buy an RV, and park it in the grandchildren's driveway. You may expect to retire to the woods and not leave anyone a forwarding address. Whatever your choice, talk about it.

"My dream, after I retired, was to settle down in a cabin in the woods. A cabin with no phone," Colonel Page clarified. But his dream of being a hermit was not shared by his wife. She wanted to live in a city surrounded by her kids and grandkids. Their dreams were worlds apart. Someone had to give, and Colonel Page chose to live his wife's dream.

"She followed me around my entire Air Force career," he said. "So I thought the least I could do was let her pick where we retired." Not every day is sunshine, he warns. "It was an easier promise to make than to live. But we had to move a lot for my career. She put up with a lot. So this one last move, I thought she should have the final say."

The emotional playbook is a great tool. It all comes down to communication. Talk to one another about what you want, what you hope to have, and how to make it work together.

Purposeful Planning Questions:

1. How will an emotional playbook help in your retirement?

2. Are there other topics specific to your circumstances which should be included in your emotional playbook?

3. Pick a topic in the emotional playbook to discuss with your partner today.

Chapter 8

Reaching Out

H umans are social creatures. We need to feel connected. It's in our very DNA and the reason we have survived.

When you're retired, feeling that same level of connection can be harder. You are no longer surrounded by coworkers and colleagues. At times, this can be great! You can be selective about the people you want in your life. But with the positive also comes the negative. You may also lose touch with wonderful people.

"I miss the people," a friend recently told me when we were talking about his retirement. He did not miss the problems. He did not miss the stress. But he missed the relationships. Those, he found, were harder to leave behind.

THE SENILITY PRAYER:
Grant me the senility to forget the people I never
liked anyway, the good fortune to run into the ones
I do, and the eyesight to tell the difference.

According to a study conducted by researchers from the University of California, San Francisco, 43 percent of seniors reported feeling lonely on a regular basis. Ironically, loneliness has nothing to do with whether we live alone or are surrounded by a spouse, children, or grandchildren, although almost half of women over 75 live alone.

We know this. We've all walked down crowded sidewalks, through crowded parks, and sat in crowded rooms and felt very alone. But, just in case we needed it, research backs up our personal experience. In this study on loneliness, they found that two thirds of the seniors who reported that they felt lonely were actually either married or living with a partner of some kind. Loneliness has nothing to do with how many people are around and everything to do with whether we feel connected to someone, with whether we feel heard and understood.

Do not allow loneliness to become a part of your retirement. It won't let you go. It's unhealthy, and sometimes it's deadly. You do not have to trust me on this. You already know it, but a quick Google search will tell you that loneliness is believed to speed up the onset of dementia, lead to fatal heart disease, and eventually contribute to an early death.

Imagine hearing the doorbell ring, and when you swing open your front door, you find loneliness on your porch waiting to be let in. In its hands you see the luggage it is hoping to deposit in your home and life: depression, dementia, heart disease, death. Hopefully you would choose to slam the door and firmly lock it shut.

If you feel loneliness creeping up on you, take the same aggressive steps. Here are some ideas on how to reach out and keep out loneliness.

Make Friends

This is a new part of your life. Just as you made new friends in college after high school or made another new set of friends after you got married, you have another opportunity to make friends in retirement.

Sometimes when you exit the working world the friends you had move on with their lives. Without the shared bond of the job you may have little in common with the people around you. It's possible to end up living in a silo of your own creation. It can be lonely, but the worst thing you can do is just stay home. You'll lose even existing friends by just staying home.

As your activities change, assuming you add new activities, you will meet new people with similar interests with whom you may want to share your time. But you must be active. Strangers aren't going to knock on your door, hoping you can watch *Murder, She Wrote* reruns together.

As you choose to be active and choose to live a life outside the constraints of your own living room, you will meet new people and make new friends. You will form friendships as you serve and work with others.

You've already seen this through your career as you made friendships with the people you worked with; I am not teaching you anything new. This experience does not change in retirement. The venue changes, and it does make it a little more challenging. But it's not impossible. You no longer form friendships around the water cooler. But you can form friendships around your service, around your hobbies, and around your interests.

- If you like to fly fish, take another retired person with you. Pick their brains and find new, interesting fishing holes.

- If you like to travel, find a friend and plan a trip together. And then actually take it.

- If you like to serve in your community, learn the names of the people around you. Be the first to welcome a new person in any setting.

The greatest friendships are formed as we serve one another and with one another. When you are involved in making a difference, you form friendships with the people serving right alongside you. Making friends is a natural byproduct of service and making a difference on this planet.

Remember my friend Arlen Crouch? He recently told me: "I make new friends every other day. I may not remember their names," he laughed, "but the relationships are still there."

By the way, as you seek out new friendships, you do not have to look just at other retirees. I have a friend who prefers to not spend time with people who are retired.

"They're so depressing!" she said. "They're always complaining about something. They make me feel old and depressed!" Don't be that retiree!

You decide, "Today I am going to make a friend" It takes more than a thought. But takes action! You cannot walk down the street, knock on a random door, and ask the person who answers to come out and play. But you can make a different goal. You can decide, "Today, I am going to contribute! Today I am going to:

· Help my daughter paint her living room.

· Pick up trash at my local park.

· Participate in community garden.

· Teach art classes at my local elementary school.

· Read books to children in a hospital.

Today I am going to be involved in something that matters!" And friends will follow from your service. Friends will always be the byproduct of that decision.

Do not worry about making a friend. Worry about being kind. Worry about being loyal. Worry about helping others. And your friend pool will begin to fill in.

Let me tell you about another time I nearly blew up Western Europe. You didn't think I only did it once, right?

When I was serving in Germany in the Army, I was a young First Lieutenant. I was responsible for commanding a missile battery with its accompanying missile system. These systems were moving all over Western Germany and were pointed toward the USSR. I believe there were about 50 of them. I was only responsible for four. It makes me very nervous now to realize that a 23 year old was responsible for missiles that could have blown up a big part of the world.

As you may understand, the very fact that we were there was very unsettling to the Soviet Union. The missiles were on track vehicles, and if necessary, we could fire them in less than 12 minutes. Of course, we knew that there was a good chance we would die if we fired. We knew that if we sent a missile into the air, the USSR would undoubtedly send one back.

The missiles I was responsible for were 39 feet long. The top nine feet was the warhead. It stuck out over the launcher and was attached to the main missile with an azimuth ring. One night one of my sergeants decided to check the warhead and make sure the ring was tight. He took a tool with him: a torque wrench. Now when a torque wrench is working correctly, you can push it down, and if all is well, it will click. In other words, if the warhead was tightly attached, he would hear the click.

He didn't hear a click.

Concerned that the warhead was loose he started to tighten the bolt. He cranked. And cranked. Still no click. He was unaware that his torque wrench was turned backwards. While he believed he was diligently tightening the warhead, he was in fact loosening it. Unfortunately, he kept loosening it until it fell off.

The nuclear warhead dropped six feet and then bounced. A nuclear weapon bounced on the ground. No one drops a nuclear warhead. No one bounces one off the ground. So the fact that our little unit did just that attracted a great deal of attention with lightning speed.

Up until that night, I had never met a general officer; that all changed very quickly.

The world around me stopped. Military commanders were going nuts. Senior officers went way out of their way to pay me, a young First Lieutenant, a personal visit. I was thoroughly interrogated as officer after officer wanted to know the name of the Sergeant responsible.

I wouldn't tell them. They weren't amused. I still wouldn't tell them. I said, "We are a unit. I am the commander. Those missiles are my responsibility. We are a team. I will take the blame."

Taking this so-called bullet had an interesting effect. If I had simply told them who it was, they would have quickly busted him and made an example of his mistake. But they could not fire me. I wasn't a career officer. They could only reprimand me and put it in my personnel file.

They reprimanded me. We put the missile back up. We reattached it. And it was amazing. As a unit we bonded like never before.

This little incident made all of the military publications in Europe. It was not how I hoped to see my name in print. But it really united us. We were finally a true unit.

After that experience, we had the fastest drill times and passed all inspections with flying colors. The word was out. "Lieutenant Smith has our backs." And a little under their breath they said, "Make sure your torque wrench is turned the right way." Strong relationships were formed through this experience. Strong relationships will always be formed when we serve and work together to make a difference.

"Preparation for old age should begin not later than one's teens. A life which is empty of purpose until 65 will not suddenly become filled on retirement."
– Arthur E. Morgan

Go Clubbing

Stacie Vittetoe has the honor of being the youngest member of the "Old Woman Book Club." The women share the common links of having taught at a local middle school, loving to read, and loving to play.

Stacie has not retired quite yet but she is certainly taking notes from the women around her. "They love their retirement. But that's not surprising. They've enjoyed teaching and now they are enjoying this stage of their life. These are women who find joy in whatever season of life they are in. Your personality and your ability to be happy does not change just because you retire."

The oldest member of the book club is 86. "She just stopped teaching tennis lessons two years ago," Stacie says. "She's also very politically active and reads every book assigned every month."

And at their monthly meeting, they make more plans. What classes do they want to take together? What plays do they want to go and see? What new trails do they want to go hike? What trips do they want to take?

"Our interaction helps everyone be happier and stay active. These ladies are sharp," Stacie says. "They go to activities. They teach classes. They are always busy and active. When they were working, they were smart and frugal with their money. We all come from different circumstances – divorced, widowed, married – and none of us are rich. But they're managing well in their retirement."

These retired teachers have taught their students how to succeed in this world, and now they have decided that in their retirement they want to see it. So they travel to China, Europe, and Russia, just to name a few of their most recent trips.

"We're not scared," Stacie said. "We all know that when we stop doing things, our world gets smaller and smaller. And you get to the point where you are unwilling to step out of that world. We want to keep our world very large."

This book club is not going to be dismantled anytime soon. As the youngest member of the Old Woman Book Club, Stacie's job is to keep them all together, no matter what and no matter who comes and goes.

"When they get to the point where they cannot drive, I have promised to drive and pick them all up from their retirement homes. We'll get together, read, talk, and eat pudding. I have written down the flavors of their favorite puddings. But I have asked that they all try to move into the same retirement home and then we can just meet there. It'd be much easier," Stacie laughs.

When a friend of mine moved away from her old job and her old community, she left behind her reading group. She wanted to start a new one and make new friends but did not know how to do it in a new location. She reached out, found a neighbor who seemed to know many people, and asked for help.

"I want to start a book club," she said. "Will you help me invite people that may also be interested?"

It took some time, but soon she had a new book group she loved as much as her old one. They meet once a month to talk a little bit about the book they read that month and a lot about their spouses, their children, and their community. And to top the evening off, they have dessert. It brings happiness to their lives. Whether you're established in your own community or just moving into a new one, think about going clubbing!

Communicate

One of the ways to keep your brain sharp is through meaningful communication. As mentioned earlier, we all experience a need to interact with other human beings. This need does not go away after we retire.

As we get older, this gets harder. Sometimes we cannot hear well. And if we can't hear well, we tend to shy away from people because we are embarrassed or frustrated. We can also be afraid that we are sharing the same stories multiple times until our children are ready to have us committed somewhere. We stop sharing because we are embarrassed and wonder, "Wait, is this a story I've already told?"

Don't quit. Don't you dare quit! Get an iPad and start writing if it's hard to talk or hear others. If you can't hear, you can still write.

I'm not the only old person out there writing. Did you know Bram Stoker didn't write *Dracula* until he was 50? Laura Ingalls Wilder was in her mid-60s when she finally published *Little House in the Big Woods.* When you were little, did you read *Black Beauty*? Anna Sewell published her book when she was 57.

You don't have to write about vampires or even about horses. Like Wilder, you can write what you know: you.

My generation needs to understand that what we accomplished over our lifetime matters. And once we understand our place, our legacy, we need to share it with those around us.

We tend to think a legacy needs to be something worthy of the front page of the newspaper. That's not right. Living an honest life is a legacy. Serving your whole life is a legacy. No, it's not on the front page of the newspaper. But it's what really matters. Share your story. Sharing is learning. It is something of great value we can give to those we love.
Keep communicating.

Babysit

If you want to keep your brain functioning at a high level, new research tells us to babysit, at least in moderation. We've always heard that spending time with our grandchildren keeps us young – at least young at heart! But now research shows us that what we've always said is actually true.

*Here is an exercise suggested for seniors to build muscle strength in the arms and shoulders. It seems so easy, so I thought I'd pass it on to some of my friends.
Just don't overdo it.*

Begin by standing on a comfortable surface, where you have plenty of room at each side.

*With a 5-LB. potato sack in each hand, extend your arms
straight out from your sides, and hold them there as long as you
can. Try to reach a full minute, and then relax.*

*Each day, you'll find that you can hold this position
for just a bit longer.*

*After a couple of weeks move up to 10-LB sack,
then 50-LB, and eventually try to lift
a 100-LB potato sack in each hand,
and hold your arms straight
for more than a full minute.*

*After you feel confident at that level,
put a potato in each of the sacks!*

Researchers from the Women's Health Aging Project
in Australia studied the cognitive function of over
180 women who cared for their grandchildren. They
found that the women who spent one day a week
caring for their grandchildren had a lower risk
of developing Alzheimer's, dementia, and other
cognitive disorders.

But you can overdo it. This study also found that
grandparents who spent five days a week or more
caring for their grandchildren may have a higher risk
of developing neurodegenerative disorders.

This study was the first of its kind to examine
the effects of babysitting on cognition. But other
completed studies have pointed to the fact that
regular interaction with our grandkids can have a

very positive effect on our mental health; it can help us ward off depression, lower our risk of developing Alzheimer's, and even help us live longer. For example, a study performed by the Institute on Aging at Boston College studied 376 grandparents and 340 children for 19 years. The study found that the closer the relationship between the grandparent and the grandchild, the less likely either one was to develop depression.

How do you define a "close relationship" or a "close bond"? They defined it as a relationship where:

- The child feels emotionally close to the grandparent.

- The child has regular contact with the grandparent.

- The child sees the grandparent as a source of social support.

If we want to communicate better and develop these stronger relationships, we have to communicate both our way and their way. Our way may be a phone call, a handwritten letter. What a treat that would be for a grandchild to find in the mailbox. Their way might be texting, tweeting, and getting on those social media sites. If you cover all your bases, you've done a great job.

My friend has a consistent date with his granddaughters. He picks them up and takes them to a local fast food place with a "playland." No one else is invited. It is his time to talk and catch up with his granddaughters.

I also know of a 90-year-old dad who gets on Facebook every day! He tells stories, shares pictures, and wishes friends and families a happy birthday on their special day.

What a wonderful gift we can receive by spending time and communicating with our grandchildren! A long, healthy life. What a wonderful gift we can give by spending time with our grandchildren! Perhaps a life free from darkness and depression, of knowing someone is there and supportive, no matter what, because we have taken the time to reach out.

Purposeful Planning Questions:

1. What new tools will you adopt in order to stay connected?

2. After reading this chapter, can you think of ways you reach out to others?

3. How can you reach out to another retiree who suffers from loneliness?

4. What will you do today to improve your communication skills.

Chapter 9

Take Care of Yourself

When people first retire, they are tempted to take a look around and tackle tasks which have been put off for a long time.

They paint the bathroom, re-landscape the lawn, clean out the closet. They get rid of stuff.

For the first time in probably 40 years, you no longer have to accumulate stuff. The race to keep up with the Jones' has turned on its face. You are now in a race to actually downsize. With one exception. A community near my ranch is dominated not by fancy cars but fancy golf carts. Retirees are actively accumulating fancy designer golf carts. But they're rationally downsizing everything else.

In fact, you are probably looking around right now and trying to figure out how to unload some of the knick-knacks around you. Welcome to the state of downsizing, when you realize that more stuff just means more things to dust and clean.

This effort to downsize and clean out can bring happiness to your life. Author Joshua Becker wrote about this in his book *The More of Less*. He has also shared how he chose to get rid of 70 percent of what he owned with great results.

Three years ago, we sold, donated, or discarded over 70% of our family's possessions. We removed clothes, furniture, decorations, cookware, tools, books, toys, plus anything else we could find in our home that was not immediately useful or beautiful. The result has been a completely transformed life and lifestyle. It is a decision we have never regretted.

Wes Moss wrote a book entitled *You Can Retire Sooner Than You Think.* He surveyed over 1,200 people and tracked their level of happiness. He found that their level of happiness plateaued at about $500,000 in retirement savings. Experts may agree that $500,000 is a rather small nest egg. But Moss showed that once basic needs are met, more money and more stuff does not equal more happiness. If it's a physical weight on you, get rid of it.

This physical clean-up is great. It's productive. It feels amazing. In the midst of this big physical cleanup, have you considered cleaning yourself up?

- Can you eat better?

- Can you make healthier choices?

- Can you set the stage for a happier and healthier retirement?

Organ Recitals

I hate organ recitals, and I believe I am invited to too many of them. Have you attended an organ recital lately?

They can be tragic events. Retirees get together and talk about their organs. Which one is acting up, which one has threatened to stop working, which one is actually working too much. Some people really get into their own organ recital. To me, they are as depressing as hell.

"I have six stents. . ."

"I have nine. . ."

"How many knees have you replaced?"

"I've been constipated for. . ."

And so it goes. If you are attending too many organ recitals, you need to get new friends. If you are participating in an organ recital, stop. Stop it right now. Find something else to talk about. Organ recitals make you depressed, they sap your energy, they get you stuck in a rut of negative thinking, and they make those around you depressed as well.

Find something else to focus on.

If we want to do well, we need to feel well. The problem is, some days we just do not feel well. So what do we do? We do not make it our focus.

Retirement means little if we do not have good health. We all have friends who are restricted in their activities because of their health. Good health is a gift, and if we have it, we need to take care of it. Old age is a crummy reward for a life well-lived. But that does not mean we need to focus on the bad. We may not have complete control over our health, but we do have complete control over our outlook. So what do we do?

"Keep going!" a friend recently said. "Keep a positive attitude. We all know people who only want to talk about their bad health. They want to talk about every single ache in every single bone. Don't do that! That's the last thing we should be focusing on. Because what happens when we focus on that ache? It gets bigger and bigger. It never ends."

What can you do at the next organ recital? Change the topic!

Talk about what you're reading.

Talk about what you saw on your walk around the block.

Talk about the next vacation you are planning.

Talk about anything else. We need to have something meaningful to do and talk about beyond what is on television and the calamities of our last bowel movement.

Move!

Have you moved today? Beyond flipping pages in this book, which I thank you for, are you moving around? Inertia is the enemy of retirees. Keep moving. You need to stay in good physical shape.

You'll be happier! Think of how you feel when you are outside, riding a bike, or going on a walk. Think of how you feel when you are playing a game of tennis with a friend or having a grandchild teach you all about the game of pickleball.

Physical activity stimulates endorphins, natural chemicals which promote a physical feeling of happiness. If you are looking for more happiness in your life, look for more ways to incorporate exercise. It will help you be happier and live longer.

The obesity epidemic is tragic. According to numbers available in 2015, over 13 million seniors in the United States are obese. The problem is so severe that the federal government passed legislation offering free weight loss counseling with a primary care physician through Medicare. You do not even have to pay a co-pay.

We all need to do our part in removing ourselves from the 13 million. It's hard. We all know that our metabolism is one of the first things to slow down in our bodies. If life was fair, the first thing to slow down would be hair growth in our ears. It's not. It's our metabolism, and we can work with it. If we exercise, if we get our heart rate up, our metabolism goes up.

We also build muscle mass and our bones have improved bone density when we exercise, meaning we don't slouch forward and we don't break if we fall over, either. But hopefully we will do less of that, because exercise improves our mobility and balance. When we exercise, our bodies do a better job at fighting off illness. We're also able to digest our food better, though if that successfully happens for you, remember our conversation about organ recitals: you don't have to share it with anyone and everyone.

Research tells us that we are also better able to fight off big diseases like Alzheimer's, diabetes, heart disease, osteoporosis and even certain cancers. It helps us sleep better, because we actually are tired from doing something, and it increases our mood and general feeling of self-confidence. We just feel better.

Grandpa and Grandma may give like Santa and Mrs. Claus, but they do not have to look like them.

This chapter and section is not dedicated to sharing diet tips. I hate diets. I always have. But I do believe that we all need to move our body every day in order to maintain a weight that makes sense to us. I believe that we all need to maintain a regimen that keeps our bodies well.

Many years ago I was watching a video of myself giving a presentation. I was shocked by my appearance. I was 40 pounds overweight. Because my pant size kept getting larger and larger, a part of my brain knew I was gaining weight. But I had no idea how I looked to the rest of the world. When you look in the mirror, you see yourself straight on. In this video I saw myself from the side. When was the last time you viewed yourself from the side? It can be shocking!

Go ahead and take a look.

I'll wait.

How did it go?

For me, viewing my side self was terrifying. I thought, "Who is this man with the gut?"

Two Old Guys at Dinner

An elderly couple has dinner at another couple's house, and after eating, the wives leave the table and go into the kitchen. The two gentlemen are talking, and one says, 'Last night we went out to a new restaurant and it was really great. I would recommend it very highly.'

The other man asks, 'What is the name of the restaurant?'

The first man thinks and thinks and finally asks, 'What is the name of that flower you give to someone you love? You know...the one that's red and has thorns.'

'Do you mean a rose?'

'Yes, that's the one,' replied the man. He then turns towards the kitchen and yells, 'Rose, what's the name of that restaurant we went to last night?

If you feel good, you have the opportunity to do good. So what does that mean? It means if I want to have a purposeful retirement, I have to feel well. It means I have to go out and move my body.

I had to make a big change. I had to cut back on what I ate. Let me confess, eating is one of my favorite things. But after I saw myself on tape, I knew I had to make a change. I still ate what I wanted. I just cut back on the volume.

It took me two years to take off the 40 pounds. I did not diet, and I am morally opposed to strenuous exercise, so I did not sign up for intense gym classes. But I did cut back on how much food I ate. And I did move my body, every day. I walked, I went swimming, I moved my body. And I did it each and every day.

Sometimes we might think, "I am 75 years old. I have earned the right to eat what I want. I have earned the right to eat that cookie" Or, we might say, "I am old. I have earned the right to eat that chocolate donut" You are right. You are absolutely right. You can eat that cookie or donut if you want to. But if you want to make it to 76, you might want to think about it carefully.

Turn Your Alarm Clock On

We all know that sleep is rarely our friend as we get older. My friend Juliann, who moved from Washington, D.C. to San Diego, has decided to use her unpredictable sleeping habits to her advantage. She cannot sleep as much or as long as she used to, so she uses the extra time to do something she loves. She grabs her dogs and heads out for a hike in the San Diego hills.

"I get up earlier than I ever thought I would," she admitted. "But I am making it work for me. I get up and get going. I go hiking nearly every morning."

I am not telling you anything revolutionary. But I do want to tell you things which may be actionable. As my friend Stephen Covey shared in his book *The 7 Habits of Highly Effective People*, you need to practice habit 2: "Begin with the End in Mind." Visualize your goal and then put your goal in writing. Understand what you want to accomplish and then decide what steps you are willing to make in order to get you to your goal.

Here's a great goal: **I want to support my body so that my body will support me throughout my retirement.**

How do you reach that goal? I have some suggestions.

Walk

How about starting with a simple walk? In May 2014, the *Journal of the American Medical Association* published a study which concluded that if you want to age well, you need to walk. For the study, scientists at eight universities and research centers around the United States recruited 1,635 individuals who were medically classified as sedentary. They could walk on their own for about 400 meters, but that's about it.

The group was divided into two: an education group and an exercise group.

The education group was asked to visit a research center about once a month to learn about nutrition and health care. The exercise group started a program of walking and weight training using ankle weights at home and at supervised tracks. They were asked to walk for 150 minutes a week and complete 30 minutes of weight training each week.

Every six months, researchers checked in and the study itself lasted for over 2 ½ years.

At the end:

- The exercising volunteers were about 18 percent less likely to have experienced any episode of physical disability during the experience.

- The exercising volunteers were about 28 percent less likely to have become persistently, possibly permanently, disabled.

In an interview with the *New York Times* after the study was published, Dr. Lewis Lipsitz, a professor of medicine at Harvard Medical School and director of the Institute for Aging Research at Hebrew SeniorLife in Boston, admitted that at first glance, "the results are underwhelming." He pointed to the fact that the education group – which was supposed to be a control group – actually started exercising. If the scientists had been able to keep the education group completely sedentary – which would have been unethical – "the differences between the groups would be much more pronounced."

Running

Remember my friend Richard Dubois who tried retiring? And did not like it. It wasn't for him. Well, Richard spent decades working for IBM. You would think he'd be an expert at computers. You might even be tempted to call him if your computer acted up. Don't. Trust me on this. He can't help.

"My experience at IBM was on the finance side," he said. "I never programmed, designed or fixed computers. And today I have to learn new technology like all the other dumb people out there."

But he does not shy away from it. "I try to be fearless," he told me once. "When I find a new area of interest, I dive in. Head first. I am not going to allow my lack of knowledge or understanding deter me or hold me back from being successful in a new pursuit."

He had a great career and will report to anyone that it was a good season of his life.

"But I had to do what they told me to do," Richard said. "I had boundaries and limits. It was a great job. I was satisfied, and they compensated me well. But in retirement, who is your boss? Sometimes, yes, it's your spouse," he admitted with a chuckle. "But, generally, it's you. You control your time and your priorities."

So what did Richard choose to do with his time?

Maintaining good health is important to him, and so when he retired he did not turn off the alarm clock. Sleeping in was not part of his personal retirement plan, reigniting an old passion was.

"No, I did not turn off the alarm clock," he said. "I set it for 5 am. And when it goes off, I throw on my shorts and my running shoes. It is my choice. I decide what, when and where to do things. And that is what makes my retirement years so much more enjoyable. I am doing things on my own and with my spouse that we have never had time for before."

> *"Those who think they have no time for bodily exercise will sooner or later have to find time for illness."*
> **– Edward Stanley**

Richard runs several half-marathons a year. That's right: several each and every year. He always loved to run, but for a season, he had to put aside that interest.

"I never had the time to run as much as I liked because of the demands of family, work and church." But in his retirement, he finally found the time to put his running shoes back on.

"I am running more today than I have in my life, and I am enjoying it more. I cannot run as fast as I used to. I have had to mentally accept the fact that I cannot do what I did 20 years ago. There are adjustments that need to be made. When you are retired, you think you are the same person you were when you were working. It's not true. You have to accept and acknowledge that you cannot do what you used to do because you have aged. I have to be content with that. My best this year was not my best five years ago. And I'm okay with that. My races take longer, but I still run them.

"People tell me that I am crazy. But it helps keep me young emotionally, physically, and it allows me to be in tune with my soul. People like to retire to the couch, and I certainly know a number of people who have done just that. They had long, successful careers in interesting fields, and a year later, they are dead. The key is finding a purpose. The key is finding something to do that will keep you moving."

Swimming

Spending time in the pool is a great option. It has little risk of injury and is low impact. Swimming:

- **Strengthens your heart.** The exercise also lowers your blood pressure, improves your circulation, and can lower your risk for heart and even lung disease.

- **Improves your flexibility.** When you swim, your whole body can get a workout, which helps increase flexibility in your hips, arms, and neck. Swimming can also help your posture.

- **Strengthens your muscles.** Every time you move in the water, you're working against the water – against a resistant force. This is how swimming improves muscle strength. The longer you keep at it, the more you are likely to notice more definition in your arms and legs.

- **Makes you happy.** I once read a book where the fictional character was determined to swim his depression away. Each time he entered the ocean, he visualized a sphere of depression floating away from him. While a fictional account, research does back up the fact that swimming can boost our mood, especially if we take a class with others and experience the added benefit of participating in a social activity.

How do you start? You can sign up for a water aerobics class. If your local pool has a lazy river, you can 'water walk' against the current for exercise. You can swim laps for a specified time. Or you can purchase specialized pool weights to help you do arm curls and calf exercises.

Yoga

I recently heard my grandkids sing this little song. It's called Hinges, and the words were written by Aileen Fisher:

I'm all made of hinges, 'cause ev'rything bends

From the top of my neck way down to my ends.

I'm hinges in front, and I'm hinges in back;

But I have to be hinges, or else I would crack!

How are your hinges doing lately? Can you touch your toes? How's your balance? Is your posture slowly caving in?

To increase flexibility, improve balance, and regain an upright posture, many retirees are choosing yoga.

Anne-Marie Botek wrote an article for AgingCare explaining that the best part of yoga is that it will take you as you come.

A senior might start off doing a forward bend by only bending down halfway and holding onto a chair for balance. As they become more comfortable in that position, the instructor may encourage them to let go of the chair and put their hands on a piece of yoga equipment called a block. The block will be lower than the chair, but will still give the elderly person something to help stabilize them. Finally, the senior may be able to bend all the way over and touch their toes without any assistance.

The key is that, over time, yoga can help you increase, not lose, flexibility. The great news is that since it is very popular right now, yoga studios are very accessible to you wherever you are. And there are apps and videos. You have no excuse.

Weight Training

I'm not asking you to go to the gym and start pumping serious iron. But studies have shown that strength training with moderate weights builds up bone and muscle and can counteract the weakness that strikes us as we get older.

Weight training can:

- Prevent osteoporosis and arthritis. As our bones weaken and deteriorate, we experience deformity and fractures in our spine and hips. Weight training can halt that.

- Improve balance. As we lose our muscle strength and tone, we lose our balance. Weight training can bring back muscle strength and hold off muscle loss.

- Reduce back pain. Appropriate stretches and focused strengthening can improve some back problems.

Weight training is not something you want to just start by yourself tomorrow.

In fact, before you start any exercise regime, start with a check-up with your doctor. While there, mention that you want to start exercising. Ask for suggestions, start slowly with achievable expectations, and set a few short-term goals. For example:

- Today I am going to walk around the block.

- Tomorrow I am going to swim for five minutes.

- Today I am going to bike around the neighborhood.

- Tomorrow I am going to jog to the stop sign.

- Today I am going to sign up for a yoga class.

· Tomorrow I am going to find an experienced, certified trainer.

Keep moving forward. But, most importantly, just keep moving.

Making Food Work For You

Remember my non-practicing expert-at-retiring, Bob Ulin? He very honestly told me: "Retired people have the tendency to get fat. Not enough of them are making the effort to stay active. They are not taking care of themselves. And they are home a lot."

What's the problem with being home a lot when you are retired? That's what I asked, as well. "You are way too close, at all times, to the refrigerator," he explained. "And you confuse boredom with hunger. That's not healthy. I will not tell you that I have not gained weight since I have retired. Certainly, I have. But I make it a focus of my day to stay active. Because if you are not taking care of yourself, you will get sick. If you feel good, you can do good. If you're falling apart, your options are limited. Take care of yourself," he said.

When we are working over 40 hours a week and then heading off to begin our chauffeur services to soccer practice or gymnastics or dance class, eating dinner becomes something we force into a very narrow window, if we do it at all. A friend of mine realized at a very stressful time in her life at work that she was eating dinner more at her local convenience store than at home. She needed something fast and she needed something that was open really late. The gas station, unfortunately, filled that need.

"Why take the time to go into a grocery store or even find a drive-thru that is still open? I knew I could run in and run out," she said.

But now she's retired and is anxious to put those days behind her.

"I have more time. I can visit community markets and farmers. I can bring home what I find, and I have the time to thoughtfully prepare what I want to cook. I am actually more thoughtful, more mindful about what I eat. I want my body to keep going and to do that, I better take care of it. I also have more time to exercise and set fitness goals. And I can achieve them because my time is mine!"

What Limitations?

My definition of wisdom is knowledge likely applied. I am not telling you anything you do not know. You know what you need to do. You just have to choose what you are willing to apply.

When my son was four years old, I told him not to touch the stove. I gave him knowledge. But, he just had to try. He had to touch the stove. So he waited for me to turn my back, reached over, and touched the stove.

Ouch! Naturally, he burned his hand. It hurt, but he gained a piece of wisdom that day. He was going to apply the knowledge I shared with him: do not touch the stove! Knowledge applied is wisdom. Now, when it comes to the stove, he has great wisdom.

You know all about the benefits of exercise. But what are you likely to apply?

At some point, people are told that they are old and are infirm. They are told there are things they cannot do anymore. You know your limitations. You know what stage of life you are in. Do not let people assign you to a stage. I play tennis with a man who is over 75. No one can beat him. He never allows anyone to tell him he's too old to play tennis and everyone who really knows him is afraid to say something so stupid.

We all experience physical limitations at different times. But don't jump ahead just because of your age. There are 65 year olds who look older than me because they act old. They are not taking care of themselves. They allowed themselves to get older before their time.

Make the decision to apply the knowledge you already have. Keep your body in shape. Be wise, but be committed to an active lifestyle. You have to move your body everyday. Hopefully you will choose to actively move away from your next organ recital!

Purposeful Planning Questions:

1. How will you derail the next organ recital?

2. Of the options listed in this chapter, what do you already do? What would you like to try?

3. What can you do tomorrow to improve how you are taking care of yourself? Schedule time for it now.

Chapter 10

Make Decisions

No nursing home for me!

Here is my plan: I'm checking into the Holiday Inn.

*With the average cost for a nursing home reaching $188 per day,
there is a better way when we get old and feeble.*

*I have already checked on reservations at the Holiday Inn. For a
combined long-term stay discount and senior discount, it's $49.23
per night. That leaves $138.77 a day for breakfast, lunch, dinner in any
restaurant I want, or room service. It also leaves enough for laundry,
gratuities, and special TV movies. Plus, I'll get a swimming pool,
a workout room, a lounge, and washer and dryer.
I'll also get free toothpaste, razors, shampoo and soap.
And I'll be treated like a customer, not a patient.*

Five dollars worth of tips a day will have the entire staff scrambling.

*There is a city bus stop out front, and seniors ride free.
The handicap bus will also pick me up if I fake a decent limp.
Ride the church bus free on Sundays. For a change of scenery,
take the airport shuttle bus and eat at one of the nice restaurants there.
While you're at the airport, fly somewhere.*

Meanwhile, the cash keeps building up.

*It takes months to get into decent nursing homes. On the other hand,
Holiday Inn will take your reservation today. And you are not stuck in
one place forever -- you can move from Inn to Inn,
or even from city to city.*

*And no worries about visits from the family. They will always be glad to
visit you, and probably check in for a mini-vacation. The grandkids can
use the pool. What more can you ask for?*

*So, when I reach the golden age I'll face it with a grin.
Just forward all your emails to the Holiday Inn!*

−Anonymous Writer

During the holidays, a daughter asked her retirement
age parents about their plans for the future. Both

parents were very healthy and active, but the daughter wanted to talk to her parents about their retirement, healthcare, and funeral preferences while they had the luxury of time and options.

"I don't ever want to go to a nursing home," the mother told her daughter. "Please. I want to stay in our family home as long as I can."

The daughter loved her parents very much and wanted to make sure they knew they were welcome in her home if caring for the family home became too much.

But there was one thing the daughter wanted in return. One tiny little feud she wanted resolved.

"Mom, you both are always welcome in my home," the daughter said. "We will make it work. You just have to promise me that when we go out in the car, you'll wear your seat belt."

Even while asking, the daughter cringed. Though she was offering her own home, she knew she was asking a lot in return. Both her parents treasured their right to make choices, even bad ones. They hated the fact that the government-mandated seat belt usage and protested by sometimes refusing to wear their seatbelt. This drove their daughter crazy. And here was an opportunity to resolve two concerns! Her parents would not have to move into a retirement home, and the daughter would not have to worry about getting in a car accident with her unbuckled parents. It sounded like a very fair compromise, but it was promptly rejected.

"PUT ME IN A HOME!" her dad yelled from the next room.

Sharing Decisions

Control is precious. My mother died shortly after we took away her driver's license. If she could not be mobile on her own, she had lost her freedom. She had lost her control of her life. Within three months, she was gone.

When you've enjoyed control and self-sufficiency your entire life, surrendering that control is a frightening thing. I believe that is why people try to retire in their own homes and avoid retirement homes – even with the promise of good food and Bingo night – because retirement homes represent giving up control.

So don't give it up. Control your own future by making decisions today. And once you make your decision, share your decision with those around you. Gone are the days when we are forced to spend our retirement in rest homes with bedrooms the size of our walk-in closet or three beds to a single room. There are places available today which are remarkable. There are a range of possibilities!

Even if you are feeling great today, recognize that one day you may need help with your daily living. No amount of optimism will change the fact that there will come a time when we'll all experience health challenges, even if it's only death. Do not put your head in the sand and ignore it.

Fear comes from embarrassment. We assume it will be demeaning to no longer be able to take care of ourselves. Our very self-esteem is attacked by the idea. There is nothing wrong with acknowledging this fear. Although there is something horribly wrong when we allow it to cripple us.

Make Your Own Plans

Plan for the future. Think about what you would like. Prepare while you can. Take control over your future by making decisions today. You have many decisions to make:

- Do you foresee a time when you give a Power of Attorney to an adult child?

- Do you have any specific end of life wishes? For example, do you need to fill out a Do Not Resuscitate order?

- Have you written a will or established a trust?

- What are your long-term health wishes?

I do not want to be a burden to my family. Today I feel great. But I'm smart enough and aware enough to recognize that at some point I am not going to be able to do things I want to do. So I am going to make some decisions. I am going to choose some options based upon the level of care I expect to need. I am going to pick out where I want to spend my last days, and I am going to save the money to ensure that it happens. I am going to face the fear and overcome it by making decisions. I am going to maintain control.

I hope the same for you. Stay in control.
Make decisions.

Personally, I'm still choosing to live in my own home as long as I can. I'm not crazy about the idea of going to a rest home, though I will appreciate someone cooking for me and making sure I have not died in my sleep. I have an idea of where I would like to spend my last days, but I am not moving in tomorrow. I am maintaining control, making decisions, and making sure my kids do not feel the burden of them when the time comes.

*I've sure gotten old! I've had two bypass surgeries,
a hip replacement, new knees, fought prostate
cancer and diabetes. I'm half blind, can't hear
anything quieter than a jet engine, take 40
different medications that make me dizzy,
winded, and subject to blackouts. Have bouts with
dementia. Have poor circulation; hardly feel my
hands and feet anymore. Can't remember if I'm
85 or 92. Have lost all my friends. But, thank God,
I still have my driver's license.*

In 1989, my friend George lost his wife. I called him
on the phone. "George," I said, "Come visit us. Spend
some time with us at our home." Well, he came.
And he stayed for 22 years. He became our Hawaiian
grandfather. He helped us with our family and on our
property. But he started getting old, really old. And
when he started becoming sick, we had to put him
in a rest home. It was the first time I had to make a
decision like that. But it was a conversation we were
scared to have with George, and he did not share his
preferences with us. So when the time came to make
a decision, it was a horrible weight on us.

Free your own children and spouse from that weight.
Talk to your kids and make plans. Fill out the
required forms. Look around, shop, and find out your
options. Go visit places. Literally smell them out. The
reality is that one day you will need help. So deal with
the reality. And deal with it while you are in control.

Purposeful Planning Questions:

1. What decisions have you already made to maintain control of your retirement?

2. What decisions do you still need to make?

3. When will you make the decisions? How can you start the process?

4. Who needs to be a part of this discussion?

Chapter 11

Purposeful Happiness

Welcome to your second act. It's yours to create.

What do you want to be?

What do you want to do?

If you don't have an idea, now is a great time to create a new season, a purposeful retirement.

Every season of change gives you an opportunity to decide who you want to be. You can take the good, leave the bad, and decide who you want to be and what you want to do going forward.

You're a little bit older but just because you're a little older it does not mean that it is too late to become who you want to be. Now is the perfect time to take stock of where you have been, what you have done, and what you want to do in the future. Now is the time to acknowledge mistakes and decide how you want to act differently in the future. Now is the time to choose happiness.

Choose Happiness

I recently read a short story in the *Reader's Digest* about a little boy who loved cars:

> My five year old son is crazy about cars, so I took him to his first car show. He loved seeing all the different models and brands and gushed over the

big engines, the colors, and even the wheels. But the car he was most impressed with was a hearse. "Mom!" he shouted, "Look at all this storage!" Now is not the time to move into storage.

> *"I slept and dreamt that life was joy. I awoke and saw that life was service. I acted and behold, service was joy."*
> **-Rabindranath Tagore**

Whatever you choose to do, whatever purpose you direct your retirement toward, choose to be happy. Choose to have a great, happy, purposeful retirement.

My San Diego friend, Juliann, was surprised at the amount of joy she found when she retired from her career in the United States Senate. "When you're working, you have all these ideas about retirement will be," she told me. "You have all these ideas about what your day will look like. And then you retire. And then it's all that and more!"

She will admit that not every day is perfect. "There are some days I still wonder what the heck I should be doing with my time. But that's the awesome part of it. I decide what I want to do, and that is worth all of the hard times. It's not all sunshine and flowers, but it's still awesome," she said.

When you are in the business world, you are in a constant state of competition.

- You are competing against people in the same industry who are doing the same job you are.

- You are competing against people who want to do the same job you are doing.

- You are competing to keep up.

- You are competing to stay ahead.

It's stressful.

In retirement, you mostly get to choose your own stress. Life in retirement is not going to be perfect. There are still things you have to deal with. But now you're in charge of your own time. You are no longer compelled by a job and its responsibilities. While you are in control, while you are making choices, why not choose to be happy?

Giving Yourself

Parker J. Palmer is a columnist and author. He is also the founder of the Center for Courage & Renewal. He recently wrote a column on the pain of holding on to something.

> Over the past decade, I've been reflecting on questions about aging and vocation — questions worth asking at any age, I think. I love my work. But with age come diminishments that keep me

from doing as much of it as quickly as I've done in the past. The key question I've been holding seems simple enough on the surface: "What do I want to let go of and what do I want to hang onto?"

Palmer wrote that he was unsatisfied with the answers that were coming from that question of letting go and holding on.

But I found that that question did not work for me, did not open onto a path I wanted to walk. So I took my quandary to a small group of trusted friends who sat with me for two hours. Their role was not to advise or "fix" me, but to ask honest, open questions and simply listen to me respond, giving me a chance to hear my own inner wisdom more clearly.

Palmer shares that he came out of the experience with something much more important than a good answer. He emerged with a better question.

I'm no longer asking, "What do I want to let go of and what do I want to hang onto?" Instead I'm asking, "What do I want to let go of and what do I want to give myself to?"

I now see that "hanging on" is a fearful, needy, and clinging way to be in the world. But looking for what I want to give myself to transforms everything. It's taking me to a place where I find energy, abundance, trust, and new life.

While you're moving forward in your own retirement, what do you want to give yourself to?

What makes you happy?

- Reading a book?

- Golfing with a friend?

- Lunch with a child or grandchild?

- Serving at a local theater or school?

Once you identify it, implement it. Put it into your life. If you don't know, there are resources out there to help you. Did you know you can go to Google and search for happiness questionnaires? You can answer just a few questions, and they'll whip out some customized suggestions on how to bring more joy into your life. If you need more direction, there are tools online and in great books on how to write your own personalized mission statement. You can even go to the library and do a keyword search on happiness and pick a book that looks educational and interesting.

The key is to act and to choose to find joy. The act of retirement is not a switch. It will not help you go from being a curmudgeon to a happy person.

Whoever you were before you retired, chances are that's who you are today.

But here's the good thing, the hopeful thing. When we were working, we had forces working on us all ✓ the time. Sometimes I felt I could not walk down the hall without being stopped with a new task, a new deadline, or a new request for a response. It sometimes felt like a constant attack, a constant force of outside pressure.

My time is now my own. Those forces are still there, but I have greater freedom to get rid of them. I have learned, very well by the way, that I can say "No!" This era of time is called "the freedom zone." It's the state where we enjoy the greatest balance of freedom, health, free time, and emotional well-being. Because we know that, we know there's no reason not to choose to be happy.

Being happy – finding joy -- is simple, it's just not easy. You have to work for it. There is no substitute for work at any point in your life, even in retirement. There is a price to be paid, and that price is your time and your dedication to ensuring that it happens.

Successfully Retired

In your day job, you knew the markings of a productive day:

- An empty inbox.

- A healthy, happy child.

- A satisfied client.

- A lesson grasped.

- A promotion or salary increase at the end of the year.

In retirement, you need to set up new guidelines to mark productive days:

- Set goals.

- Make a to-do list.

- Find out how to measure success outside of the workplace.

I'm in my 70s. But I make the same number of goals in my 70s as I ever did in my 40s because I'm still committed to making a difference and moving forward.

In retirement, you have to shift your definition of success.

Personally, I have always defined success like this: a successful person is willing to do those things that unsuccessful people are not willing to do.

You can replace the word "people" with anything else. For example:

- a successful parent is willing to do those things that unsuccessful parents are not willing to do;

- a successful actor is willing to do those things that unsuccessful actors are not willing to do;

- a successful manager is willing to do those things that unsuccessful managers are not willing to do.

And on it goes in the same pattern.

I once talked to the incredible golfer, Gary Player, about success. I asked him, "Gary, how many golf balls have you hit in your life?" He laughed and admitted that he had no idea. So I broke it down for him. I asked, instead, "Gary, how many golf balls do you hit a day?" He admitted that he hits about 500 golf balls a day. He turned 80 in 2015. That's millions of balls over a lifetime. A successful golfer is willing to do those things that unsuccessful golfers are not willing to do: hit over 500 balls a day.

Go back to our pattern. Put in the word retiree. What does that give us?

A successful *retiree* is willing to do those things that unsuccessful *retirees* are not willing to do.

May I just suggest that people who are successful in their retirement are not those people sitting on their fannies doing nothing. They are contributing. They are exploring. They are learning.

Carrie Luekenga loves to travel. She loves new adventures, experiencing new cultures, and getting to know people all around the world. She even loves to take long airplane rides, something I never completely learned to do.

A retired teacher, Carrie knew she wanted to make a difference. "But I couldn't just open my door and yell, 'Hey! I'm ready to make a difference!' and expect someone to bring an experience to me," she shared. "I needed help."

She applied for a grant and travelled to India with 18 other volunteers through a program with *Women In Need*. "I didn't know a single soul, but I was thrilled!"

Carrie taught hygiene basics, some English greetings, built public toilets, and loved the people. She even taught a few country line dances. As a retired school teacher, she especially loved working with the children of India.

"I was able to go to the government hospital. I sat with the children and played games with the terminally ill children. We colored. We played board games." She also volunteered her time at an Indian orphanage. "We painted that day," she said. "We actually painted a large mural on a wall so that the room was bright and not as dark and dingy for the children."

She also served women in India. "They live in a patriarchal society," Carrie said. "They needed help with hygiene, yes. But mostly they needed to be told that they are important. They are needed. They are loved. We also travelled to a leprosy colony in India. No one had ever been there before. But we spent the day with them. We served them. We loved them. We sang with them."

Carrie spent three weeks in India. "We got up every morning at 8 am and often did not get home until 8 pm." Interestingly, the program was open to adult volunteers aged 26 and under. Carried had to fight for a spot by meeting with them personally and proving she was up to the task.

"And when it was over," Carrie shared, "they admitted that they needed to rethink their age requirement. Seniors add experience and a different flare to service. And we're tougher than we look."

Ask yourself: what are successful retirees doing? Am I willing to do that?

What are you willing to do to experience a purposeful retirement? What expectations do you have for yourself? How are you scripting your second act?

My Happiness

What is the source of your happiness? Only you can answer that question. The only thing I can guarantee is that being bored is not anyone's source of happiness.

Happy retirees are reading.

Happy retirees are volunteering.

Happy retirees are driving fancy golf carts to their next Bingo game.

I live in a warm climate. I see retirees buzz about me on their golf carts on the way to their next Bingo game. Personally, that lifestyle gives me hives.

But if it makes you happy, do it! And be happy in that choice. But never sit there, play Bingo, and think that your life sucks. That behavior will never meet your needs over time.

My wife Gail looks at retirement as a continuation of our adventure. "I sometimes wonder, am I really retired?" she told me. "We are too busy to be really retired." Service opportunities in the community and family expectations keep us moving. Soccer games! Track meets! There's always a new adventure.

"Retirement is an age to do new things," she'll tell you. "It's a different time, a different season. You fall into that season, and you learn to love it," she said.

"I love where we are," she shared. "It's a dream come true."

We are living a dream. I am certainly living the dream. And I am living a purposeful retirement. I wish the same adventure for you.

Purposeful Planning Questions:

1. What makes you happy? Where do you feel joy?

2. How can you incorporate more joy into your purposeful retirement?

3. What can you do right now to find more joy?

Afterword

The Rest of Your Life Can Be the Best of Your Life

The British have a saying, "Who is she when she's at home?"

This idiom from across the pond points to something very important – we show different faces to the world. In recent decades, we spend more time at the office than anywhere. Thus, the face you show at work is very closely tied to your sense of self. Most of us spend around 50 years working, and whether you climbed the corporate ladder or spent your days at a trade you love, working life is deeply encoded in your identity.

There is also a social aspect, with friendships, rites of passage, shared goals, and close bonds from shared successes. No doubt you know the names of your coworkers' children, spouses, and maybe even their pets from lunchtime chats over the years. They, in turn, know about your hopes and dreams, have weathered your career setbacks alongside you and have been there for you through it all. Many lifelong friendships have started at the workplace, to be treasured and maintained long after the job ends.

It is not so easy to simply drop this side of you as your enter this new phase of your life. The best advice I can pass along is that you are still you. You bring the same value to the world even when you stop going to work five days a week. In fact, you might be able to contribute more in service to the world by giving back to others, a marvelous benefit that comes with the opportunity to manage your time in a different way.

It's all in your hands, completely up to you. You have a choice, and my suggestion is that you embrace these years with zest. Whatever you do, do not withdraw from life or sit around and wait for things to happen. Be passionate, not passive.

The rest of your life can be the best of your life.

Each day is an opportunity to improve your relationships, stimulate your mind, invigorate your body, and grow spiritually. Retirement can easily be an unbelievably bright future for you and your loved ones. You are not a "has been," you are a "will be."

Above all, be purposeful.

Enjoy all that lies before you!

Author

Hyrum W. Smith is one of the original creators of the popular **Franklin Day Planner** and the recognized "Father of Time Management". Hyrum is former Chairman and CEO of FranklinCovey Co. He currently serves as Vice-Chairman of the Board of Tuacahn Center for the Arts.

For four decades, Hyrum has been empowering people to effectively govern their personal and professional lives. This distinguished author, speaker, and businessman combines wit and enthusiasm with a gift for communicating compelling principles that incite lasting personal change.

Hyrum is the author of nationally-acclaimed books and presentations including *The 10 Natural Laws of Successful Time and Life Management*, *What Matters Most*, *Pain is Inevitable Misery is Optional*, *You Are What You Believe*, and *The Three Gaps*.

Hyrum and his wife Gail live on a ranch in southern Utah.